WEIRDO. MOS1

Weirdo. Mosher. Freak.

(If only they'd stopped at name calling)

The Murder of Sophie Lancaster

CATHERINE SMYTH

POMONA

A Pomona Book

P-024

Published by Pomona Books 2010
Telephone 01422 846900 · e-mail admin@pomonauk.co.uk

www.pomonauk.co.uk

1

A CIP catalogue record for this book
is available from the British Library

ISBN 978-1-904590-27-9

Set in Monotype Bembo Book
Typeset by Christian Brett

Printed and bound in England by
CPI Cox & Wyman, Reading, RG1 8EX

'This is a story that needs to be told and if anyone was going to do it, Catherine, I would rather it be you.'

– Sylvia Lancaster.

Acknowledgments

The author wishes to thank the following for their help with compiling this book: Sylvia Lancaster, Tina Durkin and Simon Thacker, and those who I am unable to identify. Thank you also to my husband and my two sons for putting up with me while I completed this exercise. Archive material from the *Rossendale Free Press* has been used extensively in the creation of this book. I am grateful to Sylvia Lancaster for photographs of Sophie. Many images in the book were taken by myself while others were supplied by Lancashire Constabulary.

I hope the good people of Bacup will succeed in moving the town forward and lessons will be learned from this violent and inexcusable act.

Prelude

This story is written from my personal perspective, for that I make no excuses. Had it not been, there would be no story, just a collection of newspaper cuttings and court papers. This is an account of a crime that appalled the nation and – chiefly via the internet – the world.

Two people walking through a park were set upon by alcohol-fuelled teenagers who had taken a dislike to how the couple were dressed. The attack eventually led to the death of Sophie Lancaster while her boyfriend, Robert Maltby, is still recovering. The injuries suffered by the young couple were shocking in the extreme and the realisation that we have such youths in our midst, terrifying.

But there is a perplexing aspect to this story. Why did it take the first ambulance crew 14 minutes to travel a distance of one mile – from the station in the neighbouring village of Stacksteads to the park? When the first two emergency calls were being made, the gang, labelled in court as a 'pack of wild animals', was still kicking and stamping on the faces, heads and bodies of Sophie Lancaster and Rob Maltby. What could be the reason for the delay? By the time the crew did arrive, the teenagers carrying out the attack had fled, leaving three other youngsters desperately trying to administer first aid, following the instructions of an ambulance controller.

Although the teenagers had said 'Bacup Park' when they called, the controller requested a more specific location and was told Park Road. That was the location from where the first call was made but 'Bacup Park' is in fact called Stubbylee Park and although Park Road is nearby, it is not the road that the park is on. Neither is it within sight or sound of what was taking place.

A post-mortem examination was carried out on the day Sophie's life support machine was switched off. In his report, Home Office pathologist Dr Charles Wilson described widespread hypoxic-ischaemic changes in her brain. Hypoxia refers to an inadequate supply of oxygen and ischaemia to an inadequate supply of blood. As was stated in court, the ischaemic changes were due to a reduction of blood flow to the brain while she was in hospital. Inadequate breathing caused the hypoxic damage while she was unconscious at the scene of the assault – this was when the inexperienced teens were trying to render first aid. Had trained paramedics treated her minutes sooner, could it have made a difference to the outcome?

Twenty-year-old Sophie and Rob, 21, had been dating for nearly three years and shared a flat in the town centre of Bacup, Lancashire. They were set upon because they looked different; they didn't wear the Bacup 'uniform' of tracksuit bottoms, trainers and sports label tops. Marks on the faces of both Sophie and Rob bore imprints of the trainers used to stamp on them. They were left in comas. Thirteen days later, the investigation was to become a murder inquiry when doctors told the family that Sophie would never recover. The machinery that was keeping her alive was switched off.

Whether the paramedics could have saved Sophie had they arrived sooner, it is impossible to say. However, had they got to Stubbylee Park more quickly, there is a strong possibility the ambulance crew would have seen the attack. Those paramedics would have been adult witnesses and offered evidence to identify the attackers. Perhaps arrests would have been made earlier to give the police better forensic evidence. When it came to court, one teenager admitted killing her, another was convicted of her murder (after a lengthy trial) and the remaining three had the murder charges dropped. All five admitted assaulting Rob Maltby.

The attack on Rob and Sophie is one I will never forget. I have lived with the story. Sophie was not related to me, nor was the couple personal friends. I was just a reporter but there are times in this job when you cover such an incident, which has had such major implications, and you struggle not to become, and feel, personally involved.

Catherine Smyth, July 2010.

Timeline

Friday, August 10 2007

9pm: Sophie Lancaster and Rob Maltby visit their friend
Jonathan Smethurst's home in Britannia, Bacup, for
a drink, a chat and to watch television.
Ryan Herbert, Brendan Harris and Daniel Mallett
have been together at the multi-use games area known
as The Cage in Stacksteads where they drink lager,
peach schnapps and cider.

10pm: Brothers, Danny and Joseph Hulme, who have been in
Manchester, join their friends, Herbert, Harris and
Mallett.

11.40pm: Rob and Sophie leave their friend's home to return to
their town centre flat.

Saturday, August 11 2007

12pm: Rob and Sophie arrive at the garage in Market Street
and buy cigarettes from the 24-hour adjoining shop.

12.30am: Along with the others the couple arrive at the area
known as the 'Fudge Factory' in Park Road, Bacup, so

named because there used to be a nearby industrial unit housing a confectionery business – The Fudge Factory.

1 am: Rob and Sophie walk across the main road, New Line, and into Stubbylee Park.

1.10 am: Harris, Herbert, Mallett and the Hulme brothers are in the skate park near Stubbylee Hall. The attack on Rob begins.

1.17 am: An emergency phone call is made to the ambulance service from Park Road, Bacup.

1.18 am: The first ambulance is despatched from Stacksteads.

1.19 am: A second emergency phone call is made from the skate park.

1.22 am: The ambulance control alert the police to an incident – message: 'Assault in a park, Park Road, possibly near a skate park.' Two police sergeants are mobilised along with three patrols.

1.23 am: The first caller, who is now inside the skate park, makes another emergency call.

1.29 am: A second ambulance is directed to the park while it is travelling between the Royal Blackburn Hospital and Stacksteads.

1.32 am: The ambulance crew can be heard arriving at the park in the background of the second and third phone calls.

1.34 am: Police arrive at the wrong place – Park Road, Edgeside, Waterfoot, and search the area.

1.45 am: Police arrive at Stubbylee Park.

11.45 am: Ryan Herbert is arrested at his home in Rosendale Crescent, Bacup.

3pm: Brendan Harris is arrested at his home in Spring Terrace, Stacksteads, Bacup.

3.10pm: Daniel Mallett is arrested at Harris's home.

Sunday, August 12 2007

1.20pm: Danny Hulme is arrested at his home, a caravan site at Landgate, Shawforth.

4.18pm: Joseph Hulme, Danny's older brother, surrenders himself at Burnley Police Station.

Monday, August 13 2007

All five appear at Burnley Magistrates' Court on two charges of grievous bodily harm with intent.

Wednesday, August 22 2007

Rob Maltby attends Sophie's hospital bed at Hope Hospital, Salford, to say a final farewell.

Friday, August 24 2007

Sophie Lancaster has her life support machine turned off. Rob Maltby is released from Rochdale Infirmary and allowed home.

Friday, September 7 2007

All five defendants appear before Burnley Magistrates' Court charged with murdering Sophie Lancaster.

Thursday, October 18 2007

They appear in Burnley for a committal hearing to send them for trial at Preston Crown Court.

Tuesday, November 6 2007

Sophie Lancaster is buried at Whitworth Cemetery, Rossendale.

Friday, December 14 2007

Defendants make their first appearance at Preston Crown Court for a plea and direction hearing.

Tuesday, January 22 2008

All five make a further court appearance at Preston Crown Court.

Monday, February 25 2008

A press conference about the case is held at Eastern Division Headquarters in Blackburn to give reporters background information about the trial which is due to start in two weeks. Sylvia Lancaster, Sophie's mother, attends, along with Detective Inspector Dean Holden and Superintendent Mick Gradwell. All three give statements to the press and answer questions.

Monday, March 10 2008

Herbert pleads guilty to murder and along with Harris, Mallett and the Hulme brothers he pleads guilty to grievous bodily harm with intent on Rob. No evidence is offered on the murder charge against the Hulme brothers and Mallett. The Judge rules that the case against them is not going to be pursued. A trial on the murder charge is agreed for Harris.

Tuesday, March 11 2008

A jury of nine men and three women is sworn in to determine whether Harris is guilty or not.

Wednesday, March 12, 2008

Harris's murder trial begins at Preston Crown Court.

Thursday, March 27 2008

Harris's trial concludes and the jury sent out. After two hours and 40 minutes they return a unanimous guilty verdict.

Monday, April 28 2008

All five are sentenced at Preston Crown Court. Harris and Herbert are given double life sentences for murdering Sophie and inflicting grievous bodily harm on Rob. Harris must serve a minimum of 18 years while Herbert, 16 years and three months. Both were given concurrent life sentences of five years and 10 months for the attack on Rob. Joseph and Danny Hulme are sentenced to be detained for public protection and must serve a minimum of five years and 10 months for their part in Rob's attack, and Mallett to be detained for public protection and must serve a minimum of four years and four months.

Tuesday, October 7 2008

All five appeal their sentences at the Court of Appeal in London.

Tuesday, October 29 2008

Appeal court reduces Herbert's sentence by nine months but the three judges refuse the appeals by the other four.

I

I will never forget that phone call.

"Something's happened at Bacup Park, Catherine. I don't know what, but there was a lot of police and men wearing white overalls."

When my friend rang on the evening of Sunday August 12 2007, I knew it must be serious; she would never ring me at home on a Sunday had it not been.

My husband was visiting his parents in Scotland with our older son. Even though it was 7 pm, I told his little brother that we were going to play in Stubbylee Park – that's the park's proper name and was a place we often frequented as a family. I took my camera along in case I wanted to take any pictures.

'A lot of police and men in white overalls.' I had been a journalist for far too long not to understand the implications of what she had described. She also said that the garage in Market Street, Bacup – about half-a-mile from the park – had been sealed off with police tape on the Saturday and a lot of police cars had been seen in nearby Rockcliffe Avenue, again a short walk from the park.

My bemused four-year-old jumped into his car seat and accepted our trip as a little adventure. He never thought to question his mother about going out to play at such a late hour.

Once at Stubbylee, we followed the main path that goes past the skate park. It was a pleasant summer evening but there were no youngsters on the ramps riding their skateboards or bikes, which was unusual. I didn't think anything of it because, at that time, I wasn't sure where the incident had taken place.

As we walked and chatted, I looked around. I suppose I was playing amateur detective, trying to find a clue as to what this 'major incident' was to attract so many police officers. Could I see or sense anything? No, nothing. No police standing guard, no telltale blue and white crime scene tape and no evidence of anything untoward having happened. It was less than 48 hours since the incident but there was nothing to be seen.

We followed our usual route and walked down the tree-lined path towards the many steps that had to be carefully navigated into an area known as Fairy Dell. We walked along the slippery path which follows a small brook with its picturesque tiny waterfalls, and then up the steps to the duck pond. We said hello to the rabbits, guinea pigs, budgies and finches hidden away behind the mesh fences. Eventually, as we always did on a trip to Stubbylee, we made our way into the children's playground. There, although it was getting chilly, my youngster played on everything and his doting mum took lots of photographs: I thought I had better justify having the camera.

The park was very quiet and I can't recall seeing many people about – this was strange for a Sunday evening in August. We stayed until about 8 pm but then the cold night air and the midges forced us to head home.

Later, once my son was safely tucked up in bed, my quest for information began. I scoured web sites and listened to the radio. I checked newspaper sites and online forums. I looked on Teletext and Ceefax but couldn't find any mention of Stubbylee Park, Bacup, Lancashire, or anything. So what exactly had gone

The gates into the park.

on? I was determined that I was going to find something out –
but not that night, it seemed.

The next morning, Monday August 13, what had happened
became hideously clear. As always, I awoke to my radio alarm
and BBC Radio Lancashire came blaring out. I listened to the

7am news and heard a chilling tale about a young couple beaten close to death in that very same park where we had been the night before.

At the time I was news editor of the *Rossendale Free Press*, the sole weekly paper covering this area of Lancashire. We had a rota and that week my colleague Jenny Brookfield was on 'calls'. This involved her making the routine inquiries to police, fire and ambulance through the day, as well as attending a weekly crime conference. Although the incident happened in Bacup, which was my 'patch', because it involved the police then responsibility for sourcing the details fell to the duty reporter. As such, I immediately relayed to Jenny what I knew. I told her about the item on the radio news bulletin and Jenny explained that there had been a short message posted on Lancashire Police's Voicebank relating to an incident at Stubbylee. Voicebank is an ongoing message-feed continually updated by press officers and senior police officers. It provides invaluable information for journalists about any incidents that have taken place across Lancashire Constabulary's area and saves officers being nagged by calls from different media all asking the age-old reporters' question: 'Has anything been going on?'

Jenny explained that the log had given basic details of the attack, the time – early hours on the Saturday, and the location: Stubbylee Park, but no names of the victims. We deduced that the Voicebank statement had been the source for the story I had woken up to on the radio station's 7am news. I instructed Jenny that we would need more information than the police were providing at present before the paper was published on Friday.

As I started my usual Monday chore of going through and mostly deleting the scores of e-mails sent to my computer since I had left the office the previous Friday, my phone rang. It was Nigel Lancashire, a former reporter at the *Free Press*, now working in PR. After exchanging pleasantries, he moved on to the reason for his call. He was the uncle of Rob Maltby, one of the victims of the incident in Stubbylee Park.

"Sophie and Rob are in comas and both on life support machines and Rob has bleeding on his brain."

It transpired that as well as being related, Nigel and Rob were also good friends with shared interests. Rob, Sophie, Nigel and his wife Nikki often socialised together. Nigel's journalistic background meant he knew exactly the information a newspaper needed and he told my colleague what had happened in the park that night. He explained how Rob was a former pupil at Bacup and Rawtenstall Grammar School and had gone on to study art in Manchester. Sophie had attended Haslingden High School but was on a gap year. He also provided photographs for use in the article, which was printed in the August 17 edition, the first after the incident.

When I saw the photograph of Sophie that Nigel e-mailed, it showed a girl wearing dark clothing, her hair in dreadlocks, some of which were green. Her beauty was unmistakable. I also saw someone I recognised. This was the same girl I had seen walking in Bacup. How could anyone forget her? She was so beautiful, individual and petite. I recall it was a Saturday and I had been doing the usual shopping with my children. I saw her walking in Union Street, not far from her flat in King Street. That day Sophie was wearing black clothing and her dreadlock hair was green in places; I learned later that it was not dyed – it was ribbon that Rob coiled through her hair. I remember thinking how fantastic she looked and how confident she appeared in herself. Here was a woman who knew her own identity and was not shy of expressing it.

Nigel told my colleague:

"As a family we're all very distressed. There are a lot of question marks over their long-term health. Rob's parents want to impart just how distraught they are and how scared they are for the area if this kind of thing can happen. Rob was a real mess when we first saw him. His face was swollen and he was in a neck brace. They're both intelligent, sensitive kids. They're not the sort of people to get into trouble but they have had problems in the past because they stand out." That was the first indication of the deliberate targeting of people who followed an alternative way of life.

The officer in charge of the inquiry was Detective Inspector Dean Holden. He told the press:

"We believe the victims were assaulted by a large group of people. We've got a dedicated inquiry team looking into this and we have a number of witnesses but we still need people to come forward."

Police later admitted they had not expected the injuries suffered by the couple to be life threatening. They expected the couple to regain consciousness and give statements. Even at that early stage, police had arrested five teenagers from the Bacup area and they made their first appearance before Burnley Magistrates' Court on Monday, 13 August, two days after the attack, charged with two counts of grievous bodily harm with intent. Bacup had always been known as a rough area but three of the accused were only 15 years old. Their young age shocked the town.

2

On Friday night, August 10, 2007, Sophie and Rob had been at the house of their friend, Jonathan Smethurst who lived with his father on the outskirts of Bacup, in Britannia. They had been there since 9 pm. Rob and Jonathan enjoyed a few drinks, a chat and watched television while Sophie was having 'intellectual conversations' with his dad.

"It was just a pleasant evening, a group of friends, nothing out of the ordinary. We would often meet up at each other's houses," said Smethurst.

They had each been drinking but Smethurst stressed that neither Sophie nor Rob was drunk when they left. Smethurst had known Sophie for four years. She was a friend who shared his taste in music, a girl he admired for her intelligence and confidence.

"How can you describe a woman who has almost got everything? She was a caring person and had such a good personality. She would always fight for her own argument but also praise people. You couldn't say a wrong word about her," he said.

They both enjoyed a varied range of music from 1970s rock to The Sugababes.

"We would listen to everything, we gave everything a go." This reinforced the fact that Sophie and Rob were individuals and not easily categorised. As her mother Sylvia Lancaster said:

"Sophie was an intelligent girl, always marching to her own beat."

Rob and Sophie shared an upstairs flat above a business in the centre of Bacup. Smethurst remarked how, similar to most people her age, Sophie had a computer and games console, but she also had two large bookshelves stacked full of books that she had read, cover to cover. Smethurst said Sophie's 'own beat' led her to turn up at the Whitby Goth Festival not dressed all in black like most of the crowd, but sporting a pair of punk tartan trousers. He described their circle of friends as aged from 15 to 30 and said that they too followed their own style.

"It is not what we are wearing that makes us the person we are," he said.

After the couple left the terraced house on the main road in Britannia, Smethurst went to bed because he had work the next day. As they said their goodbyes, he understood that his friends were making their way back to their flat just over a mile away. Instead of going home they went to the 24-hour shop and off licence at the petrol station. Aside from a few pubs and take-aways, it was the only place still open. Some youngsters were hanging around and Sophie and Rob handed out cigarettes they had just bought while they chatted with them. They were a sociable pair and Sophie in particularly was known for her friendliness. Later in court this interaction was described as being, 'friendly and good-natured'. The youths were fascinated by the appearance of Rob and Sophie – the Goth-style cloth-ing, individual hairstyles and Sophie with her dreadlocks and many piercings: more than 20. A statement from a witness said:

'They were being quite friendly and trying to talk to us, offering us cigarettes. They got up and started walking in the direction of Stubbylee Park.'

Jonathan Smethurst.

The witness said a male youth came over and said he did not
want to be seen with Sophie and Rob because of their image.
Was this the first sign that something more sinister might
happen that night? From the petrol station, the couple walked
along the main Newchurch Road in the opposite direction to
their home. They went to Park Road, a side road near a factory
unit then occupied by a company called the Fudge Factory.
That is where Sophie and Rob met more youngsters. Police said
it is believed that some, if not all, of the gang involved in the
subsequent attack had also joined the group by this time. As
well as hanging around outside the garage on Market Street and
the car park on Park Road, youths would also congregate in
Stubbylee Park. For some reason, Sophie and Rob walked across

the main road, New Line, and through the main gates into Stubbylee Park with a group of about five teenagers aged 14–16. Jonathan Smethurst said that it was not unusual for the couple to walk late at night because they enjoyed that time of day. Others have struggled to explain why they entered the park.

Sporadic lampposts would have lit dimly the main path through the historic park. As the couple neared the skate park, with its high wire mesh fence, a street light at the entrance offered an orange glow; the timer floodlights had long gone off. The skate park was well used by skateboarders and cyclists during the day but at night-time it became a meeting place for teenagers. Several of the lads at the skate park had met up earlier at the fenced-in ball games area known as 'the cage' behind the Rose 'n' Bowl pub in the nearby village of Stacksteads. This was introduced by a community organisation to give youngsters somewhere to play and stop them congregating near the main road. Some had consumed a cocktail of lager, cider and schnapps. Police reported later that a bottle of Lambrini was found with fingerprints traced to Ryan Herbert, who eventually admitted Sophie's murder. Although when later arrested there was no evidence of drugs, police said Ryan Herbert and Brendan Harris were known to regularly smoke cannabis.

The alcohol swam around their young bodies, making them cocky and confident. A short while before the attack, Herbert had bragged that he had taken a girl's virginity in the park. The sex with a 16-year-old girl had been consensual but had caused her to bleed. Harris too had been indulging in open-air sex, again consensual and with another 16-year-old.

3

In the early hours of the morning most children are asleep in their beds, but people have said there were several primary schoolchildren in Stubbylee Park on Saturday August 11.

Many young teenagers from Bacup gave witness statements to the police and in those statements five of their peer group were implicated in the attack. They were Ryan Stephen Herbert (15) of Rosendale Crescent, Bacup; Brendan Desmond Harris (15) of Spring Terrace, Stacksteads; Daniel Anthony Parker Mallett (17) of Rockcliffe Avenue, Bacup; Danny Hulme (15) and his older brother Joseph Harold Michael Hulme (16) of Landgate, a travellers' site in Shawforth, Rossendale, where their parents had given them their own 'accommodation' near to their static caravan.

Joseph Hulme was a former pupil of the popular high-achieving Bacup and Rawtenstall Grammar School (BRGS) in Waterfoot. He had passed 9.5 GCSEs at grade C or above but rather than stay on for A levels he chose to study at Myerscough College, near Garstang. Fellow pupils at BRGS said Hulme was the leader of a gang that operated in the school. The Hulmes' parents, Marina and Harold, attended each court appearance.

Detective Inspector Dean Holden described Ryan Herbert as, 'a local menace'. A pupil at the All Saints Catholic Language

College in Rawtenstall, he was a key player in the Bacup Terror Group, a gang whose tag is still visible on buildings in the town. At school he was known as someone to be avoided. A former pupil at his primary school – St Mary's on the large former council estate in Bacup where he lived, said Herbert would pick on the vulnerable, those children without siblings who were easy targets. By all accounts his behaviour didn't improve at high school. There were many Herberts in Bacup, but from a very young age it was evident Ryan, known as 'Peanut', was going to be the most notorious. Christine Herbert, a single parent, brought up her four children on the estate. A social landlord, Green Vale Homes, manages the former council houses. Unlike the council or a private company, a social landlord is a not-for-profit organisation that can bid for direct funding from the government to improve properties. Millions has been ploughed into improving the quality of the homes but the area struggles to leave behind its rough image.

"Make sure you lock your car doors or it might not be there when you get back," reporters would say as colleagues headed out on a job in that area. Christine Herbert was approached by many members of the press but refused to speak to anyone.

Brendan Harris had recently been transferred from Whitworth High School to Fearns Community Sports College. He was not as well known locally as the other three. The same as Herbert, Harris was brought up by his single mother, Martine Harris, also known as Martine McGuinn, who also had an older son. From a young age both boys were seen in pubs with their mother.

Daniel Mallett was a former pupil at All Saints Catholic Language College, Rawtenstall, and as a primary pupil attended Bacup's St Mary's. He had gained six good grade GCSEs. A few months older than Herbert, whether they mixed at school or how much they knew each other is uncertain. He seems to have been the person least expected to be involved in a crime of this nature, although others have said he was staying out until the small hours at 14 and had violent tendencies. He came from a residential area of Bacup, a small road of red brick and stone-built semis and small terraces. His parents had divorced when he was young. He lived with his mother Tracy, but still saw his dentist father on a regular basis.

Finally there was Danny Hulme. He seems to have been under the influence of his older brother Joseph. He too had been a pupil at Fearns.

When Sophie and Rob walked into the skate park they encountered not only these five youths but also at least a dozen others who were chatty, friendly and fascinated with the couple's appearance, especially Sophie. One girl was even said to have had her photograph taken with Sophie on her mobile phone. The picture has never been located. Then the scene turned ugly. Witnesses heard the five who attacked Rob say, "Should we start on them?" "Shall we batter him?" "Let's beat him up." A 16-year-old who gave a statement to the police said he heard one of the gang saying: "We'll bang them."

Harris was first to strike Rob, on the head. Some say it was a kick; he claimed it was with his fist. When all five had kicked, punched and stamped Rob to the ground, the court was told witnesses reported seeing Herbert and Harris attack Sophie as she cradled her boyfriend's head.

4

The gang of five quickly departed the park. Herbert bumped into two 15-year-olds at the nearby Fudge Factory and police said he bragged:

"There's two Moshers nearly dead up Bacup Park."

They met up with another witness who had gone to get cigarettes from the same petrol station Rob and Sophie had been to at midnight. He described the gang's behaviour as 'giddy, hyperactive and bouncing around doing silly things as if they were boasting about what they had done'.

The witness said Herbert added:

"You want to see them, they're a right mess."

He also told police Joseph Hulme said:

"We've just beaten someone up. Do you want a phone?" He then handed Rob's phone to him.

In a police interview, Joseph Hulme claimed another lad in the park had offered the phone to him. He said he had a look and decided he didn't want it and passed it on to someone else. Rob's wallet was found in bushes in the park on the day after the attack, not far from the skate park. Some of the contents had been strewn around but there was no cash or anything of any value.

★

When Jonathan Smethurst's phone sounded at 1.30am, Rob Maltby's name 'Bob' came up. It sounded as if the number had been dialled accidentally while the phone was in someone's pocket, so Smethurst sent a text to his best friend asking if he was all right. Nothing came back. The next time it rang, at 2.10am, a young male voice said:

"Is this Jonny?" And when he replied: "Yes." The lad continued: "Have you got two friends down in Bacup Park?" Smethurst figured the caller must have been referring to Rob and Sophie. He answered cagily:

"I might have."

The voice added:

"There's two Moshers here and they look like they're dead."

Smethurst immediately woke his dad and they raced to Stubbylee Park, about a mile from their home. The 20-year-old found the park awash with police. He told officers he believed the couple who had been attacked were his friends. At 3.30am he was taken to Rochdale Infirmary where he identified the pair.

"They let me look at Rob and I recognised him but they wouldn't let me see Sophie. I just saw her dreadlocks and I knew it was her."

After being taken initially to Rochdale, Rob was transferred to North Manchester General Hospital.

"I couldn't see Rob underneath all the bruises and the blood because of the mess that he was in," said a nurse who does not wish to be named. "There was such disgust felt not only by me but also by the whole team. This had been done just because of how they looked. The fact is that we have all been different at some time in our lives – does that warrant being beaten within an inch of your life?"

"When we first met Rob he was sleepy because we kept him sedated. When we took him off the drugs he was very restless, difficult to speak to, very repetitive and disorientated. After that he was childlike. His whole demeanour was like that of a toddler; the general behaviour of someone with this sort of injury is agitation, but with Rob it was extreme and he wanted his mum at all times."

Sophie too was transferred, first to Fairfield General Hospital, Bury, and then to Hope Hospital, Salford, where she was treated on the neurology unit. The nurse said:

"All we knew of how Sophie was doing was the reports we were getting from colleagues in other hospitals, and, with our knowledge, we knew that it didn't look good for her."

Sylvia Lancaster got up early on Saturday August 11 and went to the gym as she normally did. She was unaware that her daughter and her boyfriend had been set upon. She had left her mobile phone at home but when she reached the front door she spotted a card on the mat saying, 'Police'. Before she could check it out her phone rang. There had already been 14 missed calls. When she answered, her son Adam explained that Sophie had been attacked and was in the intensive care unit at hospital. She hastily arranged to go to the hospital with Adam.

"At first everyone thought she was going to recover. It was like we were visiting someone in hospital who was poorly but they were going to get better. If I am honest I had inkling on that first Sunday that she really wasn't going to make it. All day, each day, I would be at the hospital, by her bedside talking to her about anything. I was very well supported by Adam, Sophie's dad John and my friend Odette Freeman; close family and friends. It was a horrible time. We were aware, from the police, that five local youths had been arrested in connection with what happened, but to be honest we shut ourselves off

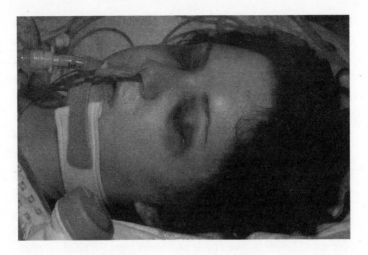

from everything that was happening at home and just concentrated on Sophie."

Sylvia praised the way doctors and nurses at Hope Hospital tried their best for her daughter. She said they treated the family with the utmost respect and courtesy.

"They also treated Sophie with total dignity and did what they could for her."

When it became clear that she would not make it, her family and friends, including Rob, attended to say farewell, and Sylvia thanked Sophie and Rob's friend, Jonathan Smethurst, for making sure everyone got to say their personal goodbyes.

"The hospital was my life for those 13 days, but on the Friday when they turned the life support machine off it was just awful."

The *Free Press* reported the incident for the first time on August 17, six days after the attack. The story dominated page three under the headline 'Young couple fighting for their lives after vicious mob attack.' The story was 'demoted' to page three because a young father had been killed in a road accident on a notorious stretch of road – Grane Road – which links Haslingden and Blackburn on the Wednesday morning. In what must now seem a bizarre editorial decision, even that story did not make the splash – the main page one story. That was reserved for an article about refuse written by myself. The story described how the local council was planning to leave bins that had been overfilled or any side-waste placed alongside. For some reason this tale was deemed more important than a fatal accident and the unprovoked attack.

At that time the couple were both described as having swollen faces and bleeding from their ears and noses. Rob had bleeding on his brain and Sophie had a piece of flesh missing from her head where her attackers had tore out her trademark dreadlocks. The piece of scalp had to be stapled back above her ear. They were both described as 'seriously ill'.

On Monday August 20, nine days after the attack, Nigel Lancashire explained:

"Rob is improving and he is awake but his co-ordination is not good. Sophie is still unconscious and was in a critical situation over the weekend. She is still on a life support machine and has had a tracheotomy, but she keeps fighting. Until she is conscious, we will not know the full effect. I saw her initially at Rochdale and then visited her at Fairfield but her mum doesn't want visitors and we respect that."

At this stage, Rob had been transferred back from North Manchester to Rochdale. Nigel said:

"He is disorientated and like a giddy drunk. He will start off a sentence and then get confused but he is improving. They have him sleeping on a mattress on the floor to make sure he can't fall out of bed. He doesn't know what has happened to Sophie. He was asking after her and we have managed to say just that she is in another hospital."

In the town, people were saying the attack had been videoed on mobile phones. They believed it would be posted on YouTube but the press office for Google UK, which administers YouTube, was adamant that footage of such nature would be taken down immediately as a violation of the agreed terms of use. Police confiscated a number of mobile phones from youngsters along with computers and laptops but no images were ever discovered. As the week progressed, the talk in Bacup was that Sophie had died. While in the town's Co-op, on the evening of Tuesday August 21, I overheard one assistant saying to a colleague:

"She's died, that girl. You know, the one from the park."

When I approached the checkout, they suddenly went quiet. From the store's car park I quickly telephoned Nigel's mobile to relay what I had heard. He told me it was untrue. He added, however:

"She is in a very poorly state. She is critical and very seriously ill."

The next day, he said doctors had carried out the necessary tests and Sophie's brain had been too seriously injured. He explained doctors were going to turn off the life support machine on Friday, but, at that stage, they were not sure exactly when. This dramatic turn of events changed how the newspaper was going to treat the story and the editor agreed Sophie would be the front-page lead – the 'splash' as it is called in the newspaper world. Even though there was no real hope for her, the story spoke of the family keeping a vigil as she 'desperately clung to life'. Sophie was unconscious and on a ventilator without which she was incapable of sustaining her vital organs; her death was inevitable.

Rob had been informed of how serious the attack on Sophie had been and on the Wednesday it was arranged for him to be taken from his hospital room in Rochdale to Salford to say farewell to his girlfriend. How much he knew of what was going on is impossible to say. Nigel described him as being 'very disorientated and confused'.

Jonathan Smethurst said:

"I was the go-between, the link between Sophie's parents Sylvia and John and her friends. We were there as much as we could be but then I got a phone call on the Wednesday. We knew what was going to happen and so we got as many people together as we could. I look back on it now and, to be honest, I am glad I had the chance to say goodbye. There is no way I would wish it on anybody, to be a cabbage. It would have been such a waste – she was so intelligent. The picture of Sophie in the hospital I will never erase but I have such good memories of her before that I can cover that image up."

A team of 14 detectives was now investigating the incident. On Friday August 24, 2007, it became a murder investigation. Sophie died on the same day Rob was released from hospital. Back at his parents' home in Bacup, he was far from recovered and required round-the-clock care.

Detective Inspector Dean Holden was helpful, immediately passing on his mobile phone number and willing to return calls even when he was on rest days. He provided as much information as the investigation allowed and was willing to discuss matters off the record, not for publication. When the assault became murder on Friday August 24, I was surprised to discover he was to be retained as the officer-in-charge. I had expected a more senior officer to take over but he said he was determined to see the case through to trial.

5

To say Bacup has had a dubious reputation over the years is an understatement. Even though the town has a chequered past, this crime was one that people found hard to comprehend. I have heard the place described as the Wild West – stretching things a little too far I think. Personally, I felt Sophie's murder was more akin to a Manchester, Liverpool or London crime, but not Bacup.

Even my parents-in-law in Fife knew that Sophie had died because it was on their television news. Thanks to the internet it was soon to become an internationally-known murder. This was, undoubtedly, going to set Bacup apart from anything its reputation had been before. It had always been perceived as a crime hotspot of Rossendale. Police may have reported low crime statistics but I was often told of incidents that people did not bother to inform the police about.

Bacup is a town with serious drug problems where shoppers visiting Boots mingle with customers collecting their needle exchange kits. Before the privacy barrier was introduced, users would rush in for their methadone prescription with a cheery 'Sorry I'm late,' to the pharmacist before slurping the green liquid in front of whoever was waiting to be served.

Flats in the town centre had a reputation for being used for dealing. While in a shop I witnessed someone snorting cocaine in one of them. The glass may have been frosted but it was plainly obvious what was going on. The drugs ingested, the lad wiped the residue on to the curtain. When the local community beat manager busted another flat he allowed me inside to view its contents. I discovered a room littered with needles, foil, burnt spoons, lemon segments, flex and cut plastic milk bottle cartons, apparently so you can savour every last bit of heroin. All this a stone's throw from where I regularly took my children every weekend to do the shopping.

People often complain about street drinking. It used to be an everyday sight in Bacup to observe people walking down the street with an open can of Special Brew, even at 10am in the morning. The steps outside the library were a familiar haunt for morning drinkers who would greet shopkeepers opening up their businesses at 9am. An on-street alcohol ban, in the main, works and the amount of alcohol seen openly being drunk as people walk down the streets has decreased. However, there have been incidents where teenagers have deliberately chosen to stand a foot outside the banned area and blatantly sup their booze in defiance, knowing there is little that can be done unless they contravene other laws.

In the 1970s the town's notorious teens had their own crew, the 'Tank Top Boys'. This gang was known for causing trouble. In one incident a gang of up to 30, the oldest no more than 16, went on the rampage in the town centre. They were blamed for causing trouble in the market, smashing bottles on shopkeepers' doorsteps and spitting over shop windows. A reader of the *Bacup Echo*, a newspaper that used to be published in the town, explained how they had come to live in Bacup from Hertfordshire. The anonymous letter said:

'We finally moved into our house in January of this year and since then we have been sworn at by numerous children, had stones thrown at our car in the town centre and to top it all, we were burgled. Is Bacup guilty of forgetting how to bring up its children to love and respect others or are the children the victims of a malaise induced by frustration and apathy because of the lack of interests in the town? For heaven's sake Bacup, save yourself from becoming another 'nothing' town.'

Pensioners living on the Pennine Road estate near to a playground known as Thorn Goit claimed they had been subjected to a 'reign of terror'. They said children aged between five and 15 attacked their homes breaking windows and throwing paint over their doors. A man of 70 who confronted the youths had abuse shouted at him, while others were living in bungalows with boarded windows.

Bacup Borough FC put on disco nights at the football club in the 1970s but these were stopped because of vandalism, underage drinking, fighting, a fire being lit and several break-ins. When lads were refused alcohol, they threatened members of the committee. In May 1974 four 18-year-old Bacup lads were involved in a punch-up in Rawtenstall and three of the four men attacked were policemen. A year later 12 Bacup teenagers were arrested after a gang fight involving more than 100 youngsters in Rawtenstall town centre when ladders and dustbins were thrown at the police. Five were charged and in court the incident was dubbed the 'Battle of Troy'.

The town's annual celebration Bacup Carnival was relocated after the event in 2004. Police clashed with youths and young adults who had spent the afternoon drinking at the festival. I was present at the event with my young family who had dressed up and been in the procession. I felt decidedly uneasy as I saw young teens walking through the streets with half-drunk bottles of Wkd close to the stalls and fairground rides. I learned of the violence on arriving at the *Free Press* office a day later; it came as no surprise. Thirteen people, 10 men and three juveniles, including a 15-year-old girl, were arrested and two police officers were injured. The previous year, after the carnival ended, 11 people were arrested. Residents claimed police were heavy handed and went into the crowd on horseback. Police said they spotted a man wanted for burglary and failing to appear at court and trouble started when the man's friends tried to free him. A shop window was also smashed in the town centre leaving the trader calling for the event to be scrapped. After another year of trouble, the police refused to back the event, without charging a hefty bill, and so it relocated to the larger town of Rawtenstall.

I became involved in a campaign to bring the carnival back, but to its original venue, Stubbylee Park, and not the town centre where alcohol is so freely available. We obtained a licence for the park for June's event and so were able to impose an alcohol ban. We even hired paid-for doormen to ensure no trouble . How many carnivals do you know that need bouncers? I have to report it was a fantastic booze-free success with only one idiot letting the side down by turning up drunk and being escorted away by the police.

As well as gang and youth violence, the town has a reputation of intolerance. It is an area where over the years non-whites have been made very unwelcome in the most appalling of ways. As someone brought up in the very multi-racial Yorkshire town of Keighley, the lack of ethnic diversity in Bacup was an eye opener.

There used to be an Indian restaurant in the town in the 1980s. I was told about an incident where local youths took over

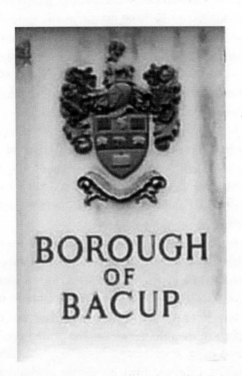

BOROUGH
OF
BACUP

the place. They were throwing plates, cutlery and condiments, anything that was not fastened down in the dining room. After every window was smashed the police arrived. Then, around 20 years ago, another Asian restaurant opened to a Bacup 'welcome'. Local youths burgled it, set it on fire and then committed the ultimate insult – they defecated in the middle of the dining room. The premises never reopened. Take-aways have been similarly targeted, some firebombed, others burgled, many regularly daubed with racist graffiti.

It is still rare to see a black face in Bacup and the older generation have been known to brag that they get 'run out of town'.

A number of Asian take-aways do trade in Bacup but the staff don't live locally. More recently the town's only remaining newsagent, Bacup News, was taken over by an Asian family, but some customers stopped having their papers delivered because of the change of ownership. Indeed the town's post office is now run by Asians. Whether the mindset of some of the ignorant and intolerant residents will ever change is a matter of conjecture.

By contrast, in 2009 Bacup-born Piers Linney was selected by the government as a role model for young black teens to show them what they can achieve. He has been a successful investment banker and now runs a multi-million pound global telecommunications business, Genesis.

The school my children attend struggle to illustrate different cultures because, apart from some Chinese children, the school does not have the ethnic mix I recall from my childhood. This is a complete contrast to some Rochdale schools, and those primary schools in Keighley, where sometimes all or most of the pupils are of minority ethnic origin.

6

Two days before Sophie's death, the Conservative party leader David Cameron was condemning the 'culture of violence' in a speech delivered at Darwen's Sudellside Community Centre. As the keenly contested Rossendale parliamentary seat included Darwen, Cameron seized his chance and used the assault on Sophie and Rob to localise his message to the Conservative party faithful. He described the park incident as a 'vicious attack' and urged the community to join with the police and fight back against crime. Then he criticised the government for relying on legislation rather that finding a way to effectively address problems. This was only the start of the national interest.

As soon as Sophie's death became public knowledge, the media carried the story extensively – *Goth girl dies after mob attack*, a neat little phrase with a bit of alliteration thrown in and they used it over and over again. Being a weekly, the *Free Press* was unable to carry news of Sophie's death until August 31 although, as ever, the story was updated on the paper's website and an online condolence book was opened. That following Friday, a week after Sophie had died, the *Free Press* had on its front page a collection of photographs of the many flowers that now adorned the ad hoc shrine on the railings surrounding the skate park at Stubbylee Park; Sophie's iconic picture with the dreadlocks wrapped with green braid; and tributes left with the flowers in the park. Deputy editor Jonathon Dillon had devised the unique front page. The headline declared, 'Tragedy beyond words' – a phrase taken from a statement issued by police from Sophie's parents Sylvia and John Lancaster. The paper's handling of the story was sensitive and well thought-out. The online condolence book is still live today. There have now been more than 600 comments added from all over the world.

A statement issued through the police from Sophie's parents read:

'We were proud to know our daughter; she was funny, kind, loving and brave. She was a beautiful girl with a social conscience and values that made her a joy to know. Not being able to see her reach her full potential, or even to see her smile again is a tragedy beyond words.'

A song was dedicated to Sophie and Rob by Irish music duo VNV at the Infest Festival in Bradford. A song was also played for them at a club night at the Royal Hotel in Waterfoot in Rossendale. These musical tributes were only the start. Music became a conduit; it was a means people used in order to express their feelings.

A few days after the attack on Sophie and Rob, Liverpool youngster Rhys Jones, aged 11, was shot and killed. He had been returning home from football training when he was shot in the neck as 16-year-old opened fire. His intended victim was a rival gang member. He hit Rhys by mistake. This turned the national media's interest away from Rossendale, at least for the short term.

7

Sophie's death angered me so much that I planned a peace march for Saturday September 9 2007. It was a knee-jerk reaction because of personal anger that this incident had been carried out in my adopted home town. A route was planned, a lay preacher asked to provide a moving non-religious tribute, and help sought from friends, councillors and pals who had been involved in a motorbike show which used to take place in Rawtenstall.

I tried to ensure the bereaved families were okay with what was planned and asked Rob's uncle Nigel to act as go-between. Admittedly I was hasty, determined and angry and wanted people to take a stand but when police said the families were not happy with the plans the event was scrapped.

Often, in the heady ever-changing world of news, a story such as this begins to lose its impact after a couple of weeks. The incident is reported when it happens and then sometimes doesn't get mentioned again until the accused finally stand trial. This was one news item that was not going to disappear; Rossendale should not go silent about what happened. The gang of five had a long time to wait before their time in court, but follow up stories kept on coming, non-contrived, created or massaged; all genuine.

The first was published in the *Free Press* on September 7 and it involved the cast of a theatre group called Xrays. They were former members of Rossendale Amateur Youth Society and Sophie had been one of their number. They were holding a concert at the Royal Court Theatre in Bacup and decided to dedicate a song, Queen's *One Vision*, to Sophie's memory. They also held a collection for a charity of the family's choosing. In a statement, Sophie's family gave their blessing saying:

"We have been approached by her friends from the Rossendale Valley who wish to commemorate Sophie's uniqueness by staging a memorial concert dedicated to her. They want to work with the community to achieve this and we will give them every support. As Sophie's family, we have been at her bedside and up to now have been unable to take the opportunity to thank people. Our heartfelt thanks go to all three hospitals that were involved in Sophie's care, Rochdale, Fairfield and, in particular, the neurology department at Hope Hospital, Salford. The care she received from the doctors and nurses could not have been bettered; they treated her with the kindness and dignity she deserved. We would also like to thank all of Sophie's friends, who along with our family and friends, took the time to visit us at the hospital. This support meant a great deal to us during a stressful time."

There was disquiet in Bacup. People were concerned that no formal murder charges had yet been put to the five who at that stage were accused of GBH. This view was echoed by several of my contacts but Detective Inspector Dean Holden reassured the public:

"We are aware of the comments regarding the work being undertaken by police. We would like to assure those people that the police are doing all they can to collect information and evidence to enable them to bring successful prosecutions of the perpetrators of this most devastating of crimes. We have every faith that they will bring them to justice in due course."

Following Sophie's death, the police rearrested the five. On Wednesday September 5 Joseph Hulme was interviewed three times. In the first two he gave quite a detailed account of what he claimed to have happened – he blamed others for the assault. He continued to deny that he had any involvement. In his third interview he handed in a prepared statement when he described a youth approaching him and asking if he wanted a phone – Rob's. He said he looked at it, decided he didn't want it and handed it back, thus explaining his fingerprints on the item.

His younger brother Danny was also interviewed three times on that day. He continued to deny assaulting either of the victims and blamed the attack on Sophie entirely on Herbert. He claimed to have tried to save Sophie by pulling Herbert off her.

Mallett faced six interviews on September 5. He cried in each. He repeated his admission of punching Rob once. He denied any further involvement in the attack on Rob or any part in what happened to Sophie. He did implicate both Herbert and Harris in the attack on Sophie.

On Thursday September 6 Herbert was interviewed but declined to answer any of the police questions; Harris was interviewed twice on the same day and repeated a prepared statement claiming that the only part he had played was to hit Rob once with his fist. He denied assaulting Sophie and blamed that attack solely on Herbert.

Following the interviews, a new charge was put to all five – that of murder and the following day, Friday September 7, they were all back in court for the Crown Prosecution Service to put the new offence to each of them. They were due in court eight miles from Rawtenstall, in Burnley. Similar to most areas around this part of Lancashire, a large hill separates Rawtenstall from the valley bottom where Burnley lies. The town spreads its many rows of terraced houses like fingers leading out from the central hub of shops. I didn't call in the office that morning – the gang of five were due up technically at 9.30am and I didn't want to run the risk of missing them.

The court was across from the town's library and adjacent to the police station and cells, quite convenient really and much better than Rossendale's court where the police station is a quarter of a mile away and there are no cells; at one stage defendants were chained to radiators. As I walked into the building, under the now standard security arches flanked by two guards, I came to the lobby with chairs down the central aisle. This brightly lit area with skylights above leads to the larger main courts, one and two. Further smaller courts are to the left and right and a set of locked doors leads to the rooms normally used for youth court, ASBO and family hearings.

I popped my head round the courtroom door, acknowledged the Bench and joined the press team, only to find myself sitting next to someone I knew. The reporter covering the case for the Press Association was Kim Pilling; we had worked together in the early 1990s. I asked the Crown Prosecution solicitor his name. It was a pretty straightforward and routine question. He answered my query by replying, 'Carl Robinson'. When I checked the spelling he admitted he was really Carl Gaffney. I have no idea why he chose to tell me the wrong name in the first place.

The murder charge was put before all five, but at that stage no pleas were entered and the case was adjourned until October 18 for committal proceedings. In court no mention was made of the other charges, which had already been put to the five in relation to Rob's injuries.

The Hulme brothers and Mallett had successfully appealed to a judge sitting privately in Chambers at Preston Crown Court, away from the view of the press and public, that they should be granted bail.

All five, at that stage, could not be named because of their ages. That is not to say that everybody in Bacup did not know exactly who the gang were and names were readily discussed in the town, but legally no newspaper, radio, TV or internet site could publish or broadcast their identities. If they did then they would be in contempt of court.

The *Free Press* of September 14 was the newspaper's first chance to announce in print what happened in court. Another full page was devoted to Sophie, the murder charges and the repercussions of what had happened. Floral bouquets and personal messages on the gates of the skate park continued to grow and another new photograph of the tributes was published. While taking the picture, I also took a video of the flowers and posted it on YouTube. I had never posted anything on YouTube, nor been a fan of the site, but felt that other people should also see those flowers. My commentary ended with the phrase, 'We must ensure that this should never, ever, happen again'.

My 'tag' was a nickname I had been known by in the sixth form at Keighley's Greenhead Grammar School. I felt confident that no one would identify me so it would allow me to remain anonymous. The video was posted on September 11 2007. Much to my surprise, a private message came through which said: "Is this Catherine? That's all I'll say, your voice is distinctive." Yes, I made the film because I wanted to speak out about what happened but I had not wanted to be identified in such a small place especially having young children. When the police community support officer who had posted that message identified herself, I breathed a sigh of relief.

One of the tributes beside a bouquet of flowers read: 'Here lies the spirit of a brave angel who dared to stand up to the cowardly mob. Be at peace dear Sophie, and forever watch over Rob. May your families and friends find the strength to endure the pain of your loss.'

Such touching words, so much kindness and consideration; not at all how the town was being painted.

8

Two concerts were announced, both to be held in memory of Sophie. Friends of the former Haslingden High School pupil planned a memorial concert on the eve of what would have been her 21st birthday. The gig was to be at a conference centre in St Mary's Chambers, Rawtenstall on November 25. Once again her family issued a press release through the police. The performers were bands Sophie followed and the plan was to hold a minute of noise featuring artists on stage at midnight to show solidarity and respect and demonstrate that people would not stay quiet about what happened to Sophie.

In the police statement her older brother Adam said:

"We have been overwhelmed with the messages of condolence we have received from people who want to channel their sadness and anger into something more positive. We have had so many issues to deal with and we appreciate their offers of support to help arrange this event."

In the same week, a singer from Stacksteads, Kelly Roddy, also contacted me to explain about a fund-raising event she was planning at Bacup Borough Football Club on Saturday October 6 with her band Cosmic Slop. The event in Rawtenstall had already been publicised in other media, but Kelly wanted people in Bacup to be given the chance to show the town's community spirit and solidarity with the families of both Sophie and Rob. I arranged to meet her at the end of the week.

She lived in a back-to-back terrace off the main Newchurch Road, not far from Stubbylee Park. Back-to-backs are still commonplace all over Rossendale – the block appears to be one set of terraced houses, but they are divided along the length with an equal number of homes at the back – hence the term back-to-back. I arrived at the front houses and made my way to the back, only to find numbers were a bit scarce; you were supposed to know the area in advance it seemed. The houses all had huge cellars below the stone path, which jutted out of the middle of the row. Eventually I located the property. It had a large extension built out on to the stone path and the door was slightly ajar, but there was no answer to my knock.

"Hello!" I shouted at the top of my voice through the crack in the wooden door. I heard a "Hello" in reply. I let myself in. To the left was a kitchen. It looked lived-in and a bit untidy. No one was in there. Through the small hallway to the right, I turned right again and found myself in a living room. I expected to be greeted by the human being that had replied to my cheery "Hello" but when I went into the room the only living thing, apart from me, was a very noisy parrot. When it promptly said: "Hello!" I realised where the salutation had come from. I had just trespassed. I was a conscious that I shouldn't be in there, having only been invited in by a bird in a cage. I shouted again. From somewhere in the vicinity of the stairwell a human voice called out.

"Just make yourself comfortable and I'll be down in an minute. Don't mind the bird."

So me, and the parrot, waited for Kelly. After several minutes, maybe even as many as 10, Kelly did appear complete with pink hair and what looked to be a thrown-on short dress. She was profusely apologetic and discussed at length her reasons for holding the event. She wanted to show the rest of the valley that Bacup people were also angry and annoyed at what had happened. Kelly was determined to show that not all people in Bacup were like those who attacked the couple. She explained that as someone who dressed with her own individual style, she wanted to show that the town could respect people who were different.

"I know what it feels like to be that bit different. I have a physical disability, I have chronic eczema [this was very evident seeing the scratches and broken skin on both her legs], and I am deaf in one ear. I have always drummed into my lad that it is good to be different and that he should show respect to everyone."

She told me her son had been speaking to Sophie on the night of the attack when she was at the petrol station at Market Street. Kelly added that her band Cosmic Slop would be performing a song dedicated to Sophie. It was called *A Walk in the Park* and her lead guitarist Neil Taylor had written the lyrics. Together, she said, they were putting those words to music and any money raised on the night would be given to a charity of Sophie's family's choice.

The following week, on 21 September, a further article in the *Free Press* named a number of bands appearing at gigs, the birthday event and the Bacup fund-raiser. The publication of that story led to the biggest breakthrough in the reporting of what happened to Sophie and Rob. After making routine calls in Bacup, I returned to the office. There, on my desk, was a message on a yellow Post-It note. Scribbled on it was the mobile phone number for Sylvia Lancaste. The deputy editor Jonathon Dillon said simply:

"She rang for you and asked if you could call her back."

9

I will admit to being nervous when I picked up the phone and dialled the number. There was no indication of what Sylvia Lancaster wanted to discuss or whether she might even have been angry at the repeated publicity I had given to the case and the events being held. When Sylvia answered I got a shock.

"I just wanted to thank you for all the articles you have been putting in the paper, they are helping to keep my daughter's memory alive."

For the first time, but definitely not the last, Sylvia's remarks floored me. She had no reason to thank me for doing my job, but I was also aware that here was the breakthrough. This was an opportunity to speak to Sylvia and maybe, because of what she had just said, she would be willing to break her silence and talk further.

"Could I come out and interview you and we can have a proper chat?"

"Okay then."

I was on my way. It was going to be a scoop, in reporter-speak. It was going to be the story everyone wanted to have on their notepad – it was also going to be far from an easy assignment.

That first meeting with Sylvia was one of the most difficult interviews I have ever had to conduct. Finding her address was hard work to start with. I knew the road where her house was but it was further away from the village of Rising Bridge, on the outskirts of Haslingden, than I realised. It was raining, damp and miserable, and I had no idea what I was going to be walking in on, but she had invited me so that had to be positive.

Her home, in those days, was a typical Rossendale stone-built end terraced cottage. There was little parking but I left my car on a space across the road, thinking it would be all right. When Sylvia opened the door she was exceptionally polite and courteous. She welcomed me into her cosy cottage, which she shared with her son Adam. The rustic home with its large fireplace, comfortable suite and substantial coffee table was pleasant. Around the room there were pictures of Sophie in frames on the furniture, just as you would expect to see in any family home. All along the mantelpiece and window bottoms were condolence cards, too many to count.

I began carefully interviewing and chatting to Sylvia. I was mindful of what I said and the questions I posed, always conscious that this was not a textbook interview. Anything that Sylvia did say, she may later regret, so if I felt she had made a comment that could potentially cause her problems or influence the case, I would question whether she really wanted to say it. I did not want to lose the contact I had waited so long to find because of an off-the-cuff remark. All the time, Adam was seated on a single chair to my left but he never spoke a word.

Sylvia explained that a fund was being set up in memory of Sophie using the initial letters of her name to stand for Stamp Out Prejudice, Hatred and Intolerance Everywhere. A page had been set up on the social networking internet site MySpace called 'inmemoryofsophie' and venues were already contacting the family to arrange fund-raising events. Sylvia outlined forthcoming events at the Jolly Sailor in Waterfoot, Rossendale, another in Rochdale and one in Nelson.

I was already aware of how her daughter's death had prompted reaction from people throughout the world because the newspaper's own internet condolence book had comments left by people from the United States, Australia and all over the UK. Now, through the medium of the internet, it had become an international news story.

"The memorial fund will be looking at different ways to commemorate Sophie's life. I would like, after the trial, to do group work sessions with young people to teach them about alternative cultures and break down the barriers. We are all human beings. We want some good to come out of what happened."

When asked to describe her daughter, she said:

"She was always independent. She was kind and caring and never had a bad word to say about anybody. She took everyone at face value and had no prejudice. She always made her own way and didn't suffer fools gladly."

Midway through the interview someone came to the door and asked me, politely, to move my car; my best efforts not to be in anyone's way had failed. This natural interlude gave me a short time to gather my thoughts. Resuming the interview, Sylvia talked about her daughter with affection, as any mother would. She also spoke with a great deal of pride about her daughter's character, the sort of person she was and how she chose to live her life, in her own very individual manner. She explained that because of the court case, she had not been allowed to bury Sophie.

"People think we have already had the funeral and not told anybody; absolutely not," she said emphatically. "When we can hold it we want everybody to know – we want everybody to come. We don't want what has happened to Sophie to be forgotten. The thing that makes me most angry is that it is seen as an isolated incident. Maybe the seriousness of what happened to Sophie is isolated, but attacks are far from isolated. Just because young people are perceived to be following an alternative culture they are targeted; seen as easy pickings because they are non-violent."

Sophie's independence was asserted from the age of six when she became a vegetarian. In her young teens she began developing her own individual style, dying her hair black and wearing a full-length black leather coat.

"It was just what she was. She'd always been different, a bit of an outsider. I thought she looked lovely," said Sylvia.

She said Sophie had left Haslingden High School in 2005 and hoped to go to college.

"She was sorting herself out. At first she didn't want to do any further study but she had made her mind up and was going in September. She had a place at Accrington and Rossendale College to do an English degree and wanted to do some sort of youth work."

Ironically, Sophie, the same as her mother, had been planning to work with the very sort of youngsters who took her life and maimed her boyfriend.

I deliberately avoided trying to encourage Sylvia to discuss the case or pass judgement on the accused or their upbringing, but she said something her son believed I shouldn't have heard and he coughed. Sylvia turned to him and said quietly:

"I know you didn't want her here." Adam's reaction was understandable because the Lancaster family had been advised by the police not to talk to any members of the press and he was concerned that anything said may jeopardise the case.

From that moment on, what had started off as an incredibly

difficult interview became almost intolerable. I was glad that it was nearing its conclusion. I had only turned up at Sylvia's home because I had been invited – she had taken the decision to contact me. I asked that terrible reporter question of how the family was coping, to which Sylvia replied:

"Day-to-day, some days everything is okay, and then it is not again." She had received hundreds of cards and added:

"You are given comfort that people are thinking of you, it has been very much appreciated."

With the interview over, I promised to ring Sylvia once I had written the story because of its incredibly sensitive nature, and to appease her son who made his feelings towards me very clear. I returned to the office in a state of bewilderment. I explained to the editor how difficult it had been and, most importantly, told him the best 'line' in the story – about a grieving family not being allowed to bury their murdered daughter. I quickly wrote up the interview and, once finished, I broke the journalist's golden rule and read the article to her. I was very relieved when she said she was happy with it.

Four weeks after her death and six weeks after the attack, Sophie made the front page of the *Free Press* for the third time, on September 28, 2007. I led my story with the line that a grieving mother was not being allowed to bury her daughter – I couldn't use the word 'murdered' until someone had been convicted of her killing.

The following week the first fund-raiser was to be held in Bacup and page three of the *Free Press* on October 5 was devoted to promoting the event. It had grown from a few bands and a football match to what was now being billed as a massive 12-hour music marathon. The town's football club was the venue and the home side was playing the Manchester team, Abbey Hey. It was announced that local players would be wearing black armbands. As a rule, North West Counties League teams have to charge admission to a game, but Bacup's manager Brent Peters sought special dispensation to allow people to offer a donation to the S.O.P.H.I.E. fund instead.

"It is the least we can do to support this event, being a major part of the community," he said.

We also publicised that a Ramsbottom landlady Jaz Gibbs had recorded a CD of songs for the appeal.

The investigation was continuing and Detective Inspector Dean Holden revealed that officers had spoken to and taken statements from more than 100 people, many of them children. They were not expecting to make any further arrests. That revelation in itself caused consternation in Bacup as some of my contacts felt more people should have been held to account. The detective told me:

"I have been encouraged by the amount of people who have come forward with information about that night's events and I am grateful for the positive reporting we have received. The park is a meeting place and, during the night, children gather there from 7–8 pm until the early hours.

"Many of the people we have talked to are young people and so interviewing them takes time because there are criteria which have to be followed in speaking to them. During the night of the August 10 into the early hours of August 11 there were probably 15 to 20 young people in the park at various times. However, not all of them were present during the attack. Since this happened we have had a lot of support from members of the community and that is good."

He also said police would be present at the memorial concert at Bacup Borough.

10

I am not a football fan but I knew I had to attend the first S.O.P.H.I.E. fund-raiser on Saturday October 6, 2007. My good friend Tina Durkin accompanied me. She had recently been elected as a local councillor and her teenage son Kieran, along with my two boys, made up our group. We all met up in a town centre café in Bacup before going to the event. As we nattered and caught up on the week's gossip, Tina had a brain-wave and insisted that we had to find somewhere in town that sold black ribbon so we could make some black memorial pins.

Kieran was tasked with the job while we remained in the café drinking hot chocolate and looking after my children. Resourceful as ever, Kieran located the necessary items and we made eight ribbons each with a three-inch piece of sheer black ribbon, folded into a loop with a safety pin holding it in place. They looked pretty good and we each pinned them onto our lapels and tops.

When we arrived at the match we were stopped by a lad with dyed orange hair, wearing a green Parka and with a fairly large red tube inserted into the lobe of his ear, a typical Goth fashion accessory. I had never met him before but I instantly recognised him. It was Rob Maltby. He asked us for directions into the ground and we gladly obliged. We never let on that we had recognised him.

On the door of the club was another friend of mine Councillor Alan Neal. The same as Tina, he was a maverick councillor and his ethos was that he was elected to serve the people in his ward, not follow the whim of a political party. He was collecting donations from people coming to watch the match and listen to the bands who were playing throughout the day and into the evening. As soon as he saw the black ribbons we were wearing, he immediately said he wanted one and then he suggested we sell them for £1 each. We only had enough ribbon to make a few but after a quick chat, Kieran and I took the decision to head back to Bacup and buy the raw materials and make some stock. We found ourselves literally running round the town centre, buying and scrounging what we could. At Greetings, a card shop, we did not need to explain much about our reasons for wanting the ribbon because the woman behind the counter knew Rob's mother. She generously gave us the ribbon. We had some safety pins donated by JD Discounts. I reckon people must have thought we were crazy but that also made them more generous.

Back at the football ground, the players assembled around the centre spot. Bacup Borough players stood respectfully wearing their black armbands, then all went silent. All that could be heard was the melancholy tones from inside the clubhouse as Kelly Roddy, accompanied by her band, sang out the haunting melody *A Walk in the Park*, specially written in memory of Sophie.

We begged the use of a pair of scissors from the football club and, on the steps outside the club's sports bar, Tina and I began our Sophie ribbon production line with our older children helping out. Once we had manufactured a collection of ribbons we filled a polystyrene tray more used to housing pie and peas and toured the ground asking for a £1 donation in return for a 'Sophie' ribbon. We even managed to sell ribbons to people who were sneakily watching the game for free from the banking behind the football ground. We then headed indoors and sold the ribbons to people inside the sports bar who were listening to the music. We made a great team.

When the police arrived, along with community support officers and Detective Inspector Dean Holden, we did not let the opportunity pass and I found myself pinning black ribbons onto the toughened fluorescent material of police issue coats. Anyone who saw Detective Inspector Holden's interview on the steps of Preston Crown Court after the five were sentenced may have spotted the black Sophie ribbon in the lapel of his suit. I felt very proud.

We all left the gig at around 5pm to care for our families, with no intention of returning. Our collection had been counted. We noted the amount and added it to the money Alan Neal had raised from donations as people passed through the gate to watch the game. Once tea was over, Tina, Kieran and I all had the same idea.

"What are you doing tonight?" I asked when Tina answered the phone. "I want to go back to the gig, how about you?"

"Me and Kieran were thinking exactly the same thing, let's do it."

I arranged to pick them both up and once back at the football club, Kieran and I continued to sell ribbons into the night. Rob and his family were there and they all bought ribbons. I chatted to them but all the discussions were strictly off the record. People were coming round selling raffle tickets but no one was collecting from people attending the gig who were basically getting to listen to free music. I arranged for friends near the door to have buckets to collect donations. With our sale of ribbons, Kieran and I raised nearly £200 – not bad for donated ribbon and a packet of safety pins. A never-ending raffle was drawn just after midnight. While the many numbers were being called out, Tina explained that Bryan Herbert, a footballer who played for Bacup Borough and cousin of Ryan Herbert who was to plead to the murder, wanted to apologise to Rob for what had happened. I, along with several others, kept watch as Rob walked into the main bar to speak to the footballer. He received a hug from Bryan and an apology.

As the event drew to a close, we counted the cash in the kitchen only to find we were around £50 short of raising £1,000. We returned the money to the oven where it was being kept in a foil pie dish and Kieran and I went back out to the gig and begged the additional money from the generous but drunken crowd. The event achieved its goal – a total for the S.O.P.H.I.E. fund of £1,000.

A group of us decided to hold another event in Bacup, this time to link in with what would have been Sophie's birthday. I enlisted Tina, Alan and local singer Jane Britton to help. The venue, Bacup Leisure Hall, was provided free and we soon had five willing acts who agreed to play for free: Midblue, Rusty, Jane's band Ice, Whiskey Chorus and teenage rockers Safety Pins. Together they offered an eclectic mix of 1970s music, punk, Irish ballads, rock and original tracks. A friend of Alan's agreed to provide the PA system.

On Sunday October 14, I fixed up to see Sylvia at her house, this time to explain what we were proposing for the latest Bacup fund-raiser. Her friend Kate Conboy-Greenwood was there. She immediately took over the discussion and I felt as if I was being checked out. She wanted to know why we were planning to hold such an event and our motivation. She was almost accusatory in her approach. Maybe she was trying to protect her friend but at one stage I came extremely close to saying: 'Let's just forget about the whole thing!'

Sylvia agreed to allow me to enlarge tributes that had been written on the *Free Press's* online condolence book, and display them around the venue. She also provided photographs of Sophie at all stages in her life to be displayed at the leisure hall. I gave Sylvia, Adam and Kate black ribbons, which were now being manufactured all over Rossendale and Sylvia even offered to help to create them, although it felt wrong asking her to do so.

"I think they are a wonderful idea. They are a beautiful and instantly recognisable and visible memorial to my daughter."

That night, Sylvia rang me to apologise for her friend's behaviour. She also allowed me to photograph her wearing the ribbon and that picture was the first time her photograph appeared in any paper. It was published in the *Free Press* of October 19. It later transpired that the campaign had also been donated black ribbon roses from the Goth community to sell in Sophie's honour, but our ribbons were already being created, hence Kate's unease. The two ribbon tributes ended up running in tandem.

A film festival had been introduced to Rossendale and in 2007 the presentation night was being held on October 26 and 27. One of the organisers from Rossendale Academy of Arts, Chris Lever-Green told me they wanted to offer a special trophy dedicated to Sophie's memory. She asked if I could contact Sylvia to seek her permission. Sylvia willingly agreed and the Sophie trophy was contested by the most experimental, different and original films submitted to the organisers. Sylvia agreed to allow her daughter's name to be on the trophy and said she would like to attend. She brought along her friend Odette Freeman, one of the trustees of the Sophie Lancaster Foundation.

The winning film was certainly different. Mercy Liao, from Chester, had created what I considered was a visual masterpiece and a very thought-provoking piece of film entitled *A Self Critical Sinner's Murder*. I am sure the title perturbed some people, including me, but any concerns were unfounded. There was nothing in the delivery of this film to really shock or cause distress. It was a cleverly thought-out script, which left the interpretation open to the viewer.

Although titled 'Bacup Film Festival', it was held in another village, Waterfoot, at the New Millennium Theatre because Chris had said she had struggled to find a suitable location in Bacup. As the small theatre filled up I took my seat next to Tina Durkin. Kieran was MC for the night and did a splendid job resplendent in his tuxedo. To my right Sylvia and her friend Odette were seated and on the front row was the leader of Rossendale Council, Duncan Ruddick. After several winning and nominated films had been shown in the various classes, he turned round and uttered:

"I wish someone could explain these films to me."

When the award was presented to Mercy she was humbled and explained afterwards that she had read all about what happened to Sophie.

Following the success of Tina's now-christened 'Sophie Ribbons', a production factory swung into action. While having my hair done in a local salon, I contacted the ribbon manufacturer and managed to secure a generous discount. I also received donations of pins and ribbon from the haberdashery stall at Rawtenstall Market and even more from Greetings in

49

Bacup. I sourced safety pins through an eBay trader from China. When I explained why I needed them, the seller Googled Sophie's name and agreed a discount.

In her eBay message she said:

"I read from Google, it's tragic. In support to your good intention, I will give you a 15 per cent discount on the pins and 10 per cent discount on the postage."

Ribbon manufacture was in full swing. Children made them. Grannies made them. A former mayor, shop owners and many friends in Bacup put them together. The former receptionists at the *Free Press*, Beryl Young and Pauline Sunderland were superstars, making hundreds during the quieter times of the day. Their colleague Brenda Booth made posters and sorted out collection tins. At one stage there were more than 40 outlets across Rossendale selling and promoting the Sophie ribbons – from pubs to corner shops, town centre businesses to cafes, hair salons to market stalls.

I would often return home from work to find carrier bags full of jam jars outside my home to be converted into collection tins for the donations. News of what we were doing soon spread. The S.O.P.H.I.E. campaign may not have been a registered charity at this stage but taking a stand against evil mattered to people in Rossendale. Those sentiments were felt not just in the valley as I received a £10 postal order from Pennie Ley in Essex, who explained that her son dressed alternatively. She had read about the Sophie ribbons and wanted some to sell in Essex. She later contacted me to say she had been into schools in her area and had delivered talks promoting the S.O.P.H.I.E. campaign and raising awareness.

On the advice of a friend, I approached a local Crawshaw-booth-based structural steelworks firm, James Killelea & Company Ltd, who generously bankrolled the ribbons. For their £250 investment and the voluntary hours freely given by many people who helped in the manufacture, we raised £2,000 for the appeal. I still have my ribbon, as does my elder son, who helped in their manufacture.

The S.O.P.H.I.E. campaign had already started to spread internationally and a festival in North Carolina – Eccentrik was dedicated to Sophie. Another was planned in Brisbane, Australia, and others all over the UK including Luton, Birmingham, Blackburn and Cambridge.

II

As a rule, I am not keen when the national media come into my area. During the time that I worked as a reporter, I witnessed the, at times, heavy-handed approach some national reporters had taken. I have seen my own stories massaged, quotes made up and the gist of the story changed beyond all recognition because it sounded better to 'sex-up' the facts. I have been left picking up the pieces, as contacts have understandably felt aggrieved.

In one incident national reporters posed as doctors to get into a hospital where a local child was sick. In another, I had written a story on two firefighters who had been burned because their sweat had turned to steam after they were sent into a burning building. The temperature soared so high it melted an industrial torch but because they were so well protected in their suits they had no way of knowing how hot the fire was. Their union was seeking legal action because the officers were sent into the building. A national paper made a joke of it saying: 'As bizarre as claims go, it's out of the same kind of book as the wrong kind of sun, snow or leaves that rail workers blame for late trains. In the firemen's version, the culprit is the wrong kind of fire.' The firefighters were made a laughing stock; needless to say, they never spoke to me again.

When you work for a national, the story changes from day to day as news breaks. The parameters are vastly different when you are a reporter on a weekly paper. You live in the area, you shop locally, you talk to everyone and they all know you – even when you can't remember their name. They all feel like they know you personally and even when you want to be anonymous because of the job – the public will not let you.

Rossendale was big news. This crime was not going to go away. I felt it shouldn't and I was glad of the national interest. Everyone wanted a piece of this story. I got fed up with being asked by national reporters:

"How can a crime like this be committed in such a small place?"

They were all fascinated by this little 'backwater'. The first approach came as I was sitting in Burnley Youth Court for the committal hearing on October 18. Four of the accused were brought into court together, the Hulme brothers and Mallett in suits and shirts, straight from Asda. They were on bail and had been kitted out in advance by their parents, while Herbert was casually dressed in a white T-shirt. Harris appeared on his own at a later stage because he was late being brought to court. They spoke to confirm their names and addresses and prosecutor Carl Gaffney outlined the case. It was a simple hearing and, as happens in these cases, very little information was revealed in court. Reporters can print even less. There are strict guidelines to what you can report from a committal hearing, unless you want to risk a contempt allegation. Committal hearings transfer more serious cases for trial at a higher court where sentencing powers are much stronger. The magistrates agreed that the four should appear before a judge at Preston Crown Court on October 31. This would be for a preliminary hearing to ascertain how the case would proceed and set a trial date.

The privilege of bail was extended to the Hulme brothers and Mallett. Detective Inspector Holden later said:

"I was disappointed that they got bail, but the judge said they had adhered to the conditions set. We had a community beat manager dedicated to checking they kept to their bail conditions."

All three were tagged, ordered to adhere to a curfew of 9 pm to 6 am and were forbidden from contacting witnesses, including Rob Maltby. They were also banned from entering Stubbylee Park and from leaving the UK and given instructions to attend various police stations. Herbert was remanded in custody.

As they left the court, the Hulmes and Mallett were seen to be laughing and joking and were caught on camera by a photographer. He had been hiding behind bushes across from the court steps; his reporter colleague had been legitimately inside the building. Having seen the three in court, the reporter had instructed the photographer as to where he should point the lens. That picture could not be used until after the judge sitting at Preston Crown Court overturned the ruling prohibiting their identification, but it was 'in the can' from the photographer's point of view – and the image was more valuable than the police mug shots, which all the media would be given following conviction.

Once Harris did make his appearance in court, he too was remanded in custody to appear, along with his co-accused at Preston in 13 days time.

I began chatting to Hannah Smith, who was sitting next to me on the press bench. She explained that the company she worked for, Manchester-based Steve Boulton Productions, was hoping to film a *Dispatches*-style documentary about Sophie's death and asked for help in getting background information about the case and Rossendale as she had never been to Bacup before. I took the decision that, this time, I would offer assistance. It was important that the right story emerged.

The following week we met and I took her to Stubbylee Park and showed her the scene. It was a drizzly day; a typical autumnal day for Rossendale, the park almost ethereal in the damp conditions. I talked her through the story and we spent quite a long time in the park as she filmed the floral tributes and took footage from inside the skate park itself. Her video camera appeared to be held together by sticky tape. I also gave her a mini guided tour of Bacup, explaining where the accused lived. As the ribbons were now being sold all over town, I took the opportunity to stop frequently to collect jars of donated S.O.P.H.I.E. cash from various shops. We had several subsequent meetings and I passed on a succession of contacts but I don't know if the documentary was ever made.

I later assisted other national media including the *Daily Mirror*, who wanted advice about an incident involving Herbert and Harris prior to Sophie's murder. Angus Stickler from the *Today* programme on BBC Radio 4 contacted me and we arranged to meet at Bacup's Italian restaurant, Mario's. It was one of those bizarre situations, not quite an under the clock tower at 8pm wearing a pink carnation, but a strange encounter nevertheless. When I arrived I had no idea where he would be seated or what he looked like. I knew the owner very well, named Mario of course. He is best described as a local character, a nice chap who has spent many years in this country but stays true to his accent. As Mario's is a place I frequent with my husband and children, he raised an eyebrow at my liaison with a strange gentleman. When Angus's piece was broadcast, Bacup's bad points were displayed loud and proud for all to hear. He had visited the youth centre KGs on King Street, Bacup, near to where Sophie and Rob had lived. The local youths were their usual loud selves, messing about and being 'lairy' to use a fitting Lancashire expression – over confident and rude. He told me they were swinging like monkeys from the false ceiling in the youth club. A few of the 'monkeys' were also interviewed and their mouthy semi-literate comments proved a stark contrast to Angus's BBC voice. As usual those youngsters did not do the town's reputation any favours. Angus also accompanied the community beat manager Police Constable Scott Fairclough on his Bacup beat and he candidly explained the town's problems.

I also assisted a freelance journalist writing for a national Sunday newspaper, with facts and information on the area and what happened. I presented him with my own theory for why Sophie and Rob were attacked. I believe it happened not just because they were Goths or Moshers, but because the immature teens were jealous of the attention the girls in the group were paying to Sophie and Rob. I believe they wanted to get the girls' focus back on themselves and what better way of doing it than to attack the couple. The gang of five didn't like it when they were not the centre of attention and decided to ensure the young girls were looking at them, by using the sort of street language only they really understood – violence. Unfortunately when the freelance spent time in Bacup, he came across some of the less tolerant of Bacup citizens who spouted their racist comments regarding ethnic minorities, which ended up appearing in print. Once again the town was painted a very white and intolerant colour.

By coincidence, or maybe not, in the same week that Hannah had filmed those flowers, cards, soft toys and trinkets fastened to the railings, they were removed from the skate park. While she was filming in the park, a number of council workers spotted what was going on and word must have filtered back to Rossendale Council as the former town hall building overlooks the skate park. I received a call on the Monday to say the memorial flowers and other tributes had been removed. Once I visited the area to confirm the caller's comments, I set about finding out who had ordered that they be taken away. Park staff had been told to remove the items and council leader Councillor Duncan Ruddick told me:

"It was beginning to look untidy and inappropriate. We thought it was disrespectful; their removal had no ill intent. What I want to do is, with the permission of the family, to have something a bit nicer rather than all the ad hoc putting of flowers on the railings."

There was an outcry. People complained about the insensitivity of the action, especially as the five accused were soon to have their first appearance at Preston Crown Court a few days later, on October 31. Within days of their removal, the flowers were replaced and Rose Partridge, a resident on the Pennine Road estate in Bacup, not far from the Herbert family home, tended the colourful display. It has now been replaced by a tree bearing the inscription *'To Thine Own Self Be True'* and floral tributes are being left by the tree and not on the park railings.

At that first hearing in Preston, the five stayed tight-lipped regarding their pleas and a further court date of December 14 was set for a plea and case management hearing. Judge Russell also set a provisional trial date for March 10 2008.

Rose Partridge who tended the flowers at Stubbylee Park.

Then came news of an attack in Burnley, eight miles from
Bacup, which bore a scary resemblance to the assault on Sophie
and Rob. Three boys and a girl, all aged 15, who were described
as wearing Mosher or Goth-style clothing were set upon by a
gang of seven. Two of the boys needed hospital treatment. To
localise the story, because the *Free Press* would not normally
cover an incident in Burnley, I contacted Sylvia and asked for
her comments. She described the attack as 'appalling' and said it
justified the S.O.P.H.I.E. campaign.

12

Nearly three months after Sophie died it was announced that the coroner had released her body; it meant a funeral could finally take place. Again, Sophie made the front page of the *Free Press,* on November 1. Sylvia spoke of her relief that tests on Sophie's body had been completed and she could proceed with organising the final farewell. The date was set for Monday November 12, at 11am at Whitworth Civic Hall, about two miles from Bacup.

"It has been awful not being able to move on but now what matters is getting it right. Friends will be invited to share their memories of Sophie with the people who attend and we have picked the music: *Amazing Grace* and Savage Garden's *Moon and Back*," she said.

"We would like everyone who attends to bring with them a flower, just a single flower, to go on to the grave at Whitworth Cemetery. There is a sense of relief. I can't believe it. I was quite shocked when they rang and said I could go ahead with the funeral. I did know that the process was being gone through but it was still a shock because we have been left in limbo for so long.

"It will be a very difficult day and a very emotional one. This is the only thing I have any control over it is has got to be done properly. It will be quite an unusual funeral."

She explained that the funeral guests would be walking behind the hearse as it made the short journey between Whitworth Civic Hall and the cemetery. In an unusual step, Sylvia told me they were going to be inviting Sophie's family and friends to sign her white coffin.

"They can leave their own personal message for Sophie."

Regarding mourners' clothes she added:

"There is no dress code, but people will come in black and that was one of Sophie's favourite colours."

Sylvia had also attended the Whitby Goth Festival for the first time at the end of October where black ribbon roses were sold for the S.O.P.H.I.E. campaign and a football match was held in her memory. She told me that being at the festival had made her feel closer to her daughter. The organisers decided that some of the money raised should go towards erecting a bench in Whitby dedicated to Sophie. The weekend almost doubled its predicted total, raising nearly £3,000.

Sophie was finally laid to rest on Monday November 12, 2007. The police had issued strict instructions to reporters that under no circumstances must they approach the family. Before I left the office I bought a red carnation and pinned a black Sophie ribbon to its stem; I would never normally take flowers to a 'work' funeral. I collected Tina and Kieran who were also attending the ceremony. When we walked in I was given a script containing every statement the humanist celebrant Sue Davies would be delivering during the ceremony. In the foyer, I spotted Sylvia. Now, according to protocol, I was not allowed to approach her, and not wishing to risk the wrath of the police press officers in attendance, I stuck to the rules. I was glad that when Sylvia spotted me she came across and talked.

We exchanged a hug and I told her I hoped everything would go all right.

There was a haunting painting of Sophie in the foyer. It had taken the place of the normal civic hall picture and was illuminated by a wall light. Sylvia said Rob had painted it. She added he had also painted the picture above the coffin inside the main function room where the service was to be held.

The venue was usually a location for council meetings, but it is also used for civic, social and charitable events – this was the first time I had known it used for a funeral. Once inside the main hall, all the seats were carefully angled so they focused on the petite white coffin on a plinth; it looked so small. Above the coffin was that other painting by Rob. It was equally as dramatic and this picture bore a striking resemblance to a photograph I knew well. That image of the girl on the sofa reading a book and eating a bar of chocolate was similar to a picture I had been given by Sylvia to use at the fund-raising event we were holding in just a few weeks' time. She was truly beautiful and Rob had captured the essence of her character. Later, he gave that portrait to Sylvia.

Around 400 people attended the service, many, similar to Sophie and Rob, showed their individual styles in the clothes they sported, their hairstyles and make-up worn by both sexes. One lad I noted had five of the black Sophie ribbons fastened to a boot lace around his neck. The humanist ceremony was incredibly moving and it was interspersed with comments from her friends. One, Alex Carley, read a touching poem, which had been written by Rob. Mrs Davies described Sophie as a 'beautiful girl with a social conscience', 'an exciting, fierce woman of high intelligence and understanding' and 'a remarkable woman and true individual'. Her words made everyone there feel as though they too had known Sophie.

Sylvia and Rob were invited to light candles and Rob, along with Sophie's brother, Adam, were first to sign her coffin, followed by her parents Sylvia and John. Rob placed a kiss on the coffin. At one stage so many friends wanted to add their personal messages that a long queue formed.

The service over, Sophie's coffin was led on a bier from the hall. Rob, clutching a soft toy and wearing a black bat backpack, was among those who walked beside her as the coffin was led out of the hall and placed into the hearse. Mourners gathered outside the civic hall and waited in silent tribute as the police halted the traffic on the busy main road. The cortege left the hall, led by a piper and two friends who were carrying large red flags. The vehicle and standard bearers were followed by a swell of people who had attended the ceremony and wanted to join in making the short trip to Whitworth Cemetery. Before the funeral, Sylvia explained that Sophie had always liked Whitworth and the cemetery was in a beautiful spot looking out on to the moors which Sophie loved.

(Later, when I did a talk to a local heritage group, I met a man in Ramsbottom who had immersed himself in the Sophie story. He had been to her grave and looked up towards Scout Moor on the hills between Rossendale and Rochdale. He told me that from Sophie's grave he could see the tips of the blades from one of the wind turbines slowly turning. He described it as resembling a hand waving and he decided to call the turbine 'Sophie'. Afterwards he discovered that it was listed on the wind farm as 'Turbine S'. I have returned to Sophie's grave since and that turbine blade has waved to me, too. Her grave has been lovingly kept neat and tidy and the inscription on her headstone is: 'Always an individual, never a copy.')

Reporters did not ordinarily go to gravesides but this was no ordinary funeral and no ordinary work assignment. I walked alongside the mourners, providing a welcome arm for my friend Tina, to lean on. We followed the cortege up to the cemetery. The same as many others who were there, we had brought our own floral tributes to help 'create Sophie's burial cloth' as celebrant Mrs Davies had requested and as Sylvia had mentioned. By the time my flower along with its Sophie ribbon was cast, there was no longer a coffin to see, her burial cloth had truly been woven with a bright and beautiful combination of flowers swaddling the once white coffin.

Then something happened that made the world feel as though it had stopped still. Rob sat down cross-legged at the foot of his girlfriend's grave, his head in his hands. His grief was palpable; it was a display of raw emotion that took your breath away and made you feel as if you were an intruder. Mourners, who were slowly preparing to move away from the grave, stopped. They were unable to walk away; suddenly it felt disrespectful to leave this place, to walk away from this young man so totally consumed by feelings of grief. What happened next probably went unnoticed by most of the crowd. A man, not dressed in any particular manner and not resembling the many mourners, thrust himself forward. He got out a tiny camera and snapped a photograph of Rob. I don't recall seeing that photograph reproduced in a newspaper and don't suppose I will ever know who he was.

As the mourners made their way back to Whitworth Civic Hall, journalists stopped them in the street asking what they thought of the funeral, of the case and of Sophie. Microphones were thrust in front of people who minutes before had seen Sophie's coffin carefully lowered into the ground.

At the wake Nigel Lancashire suggested I talk to Ade Varney because he had set up an on-line petition calling for a widening of government legislation on hate crimes. If he succeeded, incidents such as the one which led to Sophie's death would be categorised as hate crimes and those found guilty face stiffer sentences. While discussing the case with police, Ade's petition had been mentioned but the officers dealing with the inquiry said the attack in Stubbylee Park had always been treated as a hate crime and they saw no need for further legislation.

Later, back at the office, I tried to capture the essence of the funeral, to paint a picture in words for all those who were not able to attend:

'In the isolated hilltop cemetery, not a sound could be heard except the gentle thud as single flowers cascaded on to Sophie Lancaster's white coffin.'

The words written, I felt emotionally drained. Covering such news stories are exhausting mentally but very necessary if a fitting tribute is to be published.

The following day my editor, Stuart Robertson, informed me that someone had complained about my behaviour at the funeral. In his office, the accusation was put that I had been insensitive and had broken the police protocol. He explained that the issue centred on my conversation with Ade Varney, and it was Sylvia's friend Kate Conboy-Greenwood who had made the complaint. I told him Nigel Lancashire had advised me to speak to Ade because of the on-line petition he had started following Sophie's death. Ade did not live locally and this was my best opportunity to speak to him. Stuart suggested that maybe I had got 'too personally involved' in the case, and I needed to take a step back and remember that, as a journalist, I was there to report the news. Yes, I was involved, but was that so wrong? I returned to the newsroom, despondent. Then Sylvia's name came up on my mobile phone. Should I answer it and face a confrontation? I decided I had little choice and clicked the green telephone symbol.

"Hello."

After what had just been said in the editor's office, I mentally prepared myself for criticism. Once again I found myself flummoxed by Sylvia's words.

"Catherine, I have just heard what Kate did and she was not acting on my behalf and it is not how I feel."

She said that she had no concerns or criticisms about my actions. Explaining that I was not the person she should be speaking to, I took my phone to the editor's office and handed him my mobile. A short time later, I was once again summoned to the editor's office and immediately asked:

"Did you ring her?"

"No I did not!" I replied indignantly. "Ask anyone in the office and they will tell you. My mobile went off. Sylvia rang *me*."

He said that she had vindicated my position and had no complaint. Sylvia may have refuted the allegation, but the damage had been done. My conduct at a funeral had been criticised and my colleagues knew. I felt like scrapping the Sophie ribbons and the concert we had planned. Later that day a bouquet of flowers arrived at the office.

"These were brought in for you," said my friend Beryl Young on the reception desk. "They were brought in by Sylvia."

They carried a card. It read: 'To Catherine from Sylvia, your help and commitment is much appreciated, Thanks x.'

13

Sophie would have been 21 on November 26, 2007. It was an occasion that her family and friends chose to celebrate, very noisily too. A collection of her favourite bands Ded Mole Crickit, Eustacia Vie and Inflight, Corporeal, 3 Sqid, Andy and Luke and Goth DJ Grimley from Blackpool's Ministry of Sound played before 200 people at St Mary's Chambers in Rawtenstall. At midnight one member from each band went on to the stage to issue a massive cacophony of noise to express their feeling about what had happened to Sophie and Rob – it was not going to be forgotten and they were not going to keep quiet about it. It was billed as 'Make a Noise'. Afterwards everyone went outside on to the balcony that overlooks Rawtenstall and the busy roads heading to the town centre. There they witnessed Rob releasing 21 black balloons into the night sky in memory of his girlfriend. After the event, Sylvia said:

"It was really quite touching at midnight and very emotional. They raised the roof and it was quite a deafening sound."

Bacup too had its own celebration on November 30. This was the event we had decided to organise as the football club fundraiser drew to a close. The rain lashed down. The fact that 150 people attended the gig at Bacup Leisure Hall was quite an achievement. Sylvia was present and a screened-off private area was created within the main hall so that she need not be disturbed and could determine who she wanted to talk to.

Hannah Smith attended with her camera and filmed footage of the event for the proposed documentary. The five bands performed for free and their differing styles complemented each other and appealed to a varied audience. Children and adults mixed and the true Bacup community spirit was in abundance. My younger son, aged five, thought it was great to fall to his knees and slide across the floor to heavy rock tunes from my youth. Around the room were large photographs of Sophie at various stages in her life. These were blown up to A3 size and had the desired effect of making sure people remembered what the night was about. Tributes, which had been written as condolence messages on the newspaper's online book, were also pinned to the walls. In one corner a table was set up with a candle and book for personal thoughts, messages and feelings. Ticket sales and a very busy raffle helped to raise a further £755 for the Sophie fund. The total now stood at £5,000.

14

Just two weeks' later, on December 14, 2007, the five accused appeared at Preston Crown Court. The 20-mile moorland and motorway route between my home and Preston gave me enough thinking time to prepare myself for the task ahead. Before I finished work on the Thursday I double-checked the location because the city has two crown court buildings, with a good five-minute walk between them.

I arrived early and parked on a multi-storey near to the city's indoor and outdoor markets. I was aware, from past experience, that there is always a queue outside the 'new' court building. So I joined some 20 plus people, waiting to have their belongings checked in the airport-style conveyor and x-ray machine. But it is not only computers and handbags that need checking. Each individual who enters a court building – that includes barristers, accused and witnesses, as well as onlookers and journalists – must pass through the security archway.

The old court is near the Guild Hall and that is where the last murder trial I covered was held. That building makes everyone who enters realise that they are there to see justice being done. It is austere, almost foreboding. Its dark panelled walls and aged oak furniture exude character. In complete contrast the new building offers little of that ambience. It is squeaky clean, pristine and with it's 'Ikea-style' light oak furniture it resembles the set of that ITV afternoon courtroom drama series *Crown Court* from the 1970s. It is almost too pleasant to be a place of justice.

The assistants checked their lists and I was informed that the five would be appearing in Courtroom 10, on the top floor, up two flights of stairs. It was a chilly December day but the heaters in the courthouse corridor doubled as seats and proved very welcoming. The long lobby leads to several other courtrooms, all of which seemed a lot less busy as far as media and onlookers were concerned. Sylvia was sitting on the bench seats in the middle of the corridor and I nodded in her direction. She acknowledged my presence. She was flanked by her police family liaison officer and friends who ensured she was kept away from the many representatives of the five lads who were to appear in the dock. As the corridor began to fill with defendants, families, witnesses and many wigs and gowns involved in the cases to be heard in the various courtrooms, someone sat down next to me. I passed a cursory glance in their direction and saw a mop of curly red hair. Later I spotted the same woman in the public gallery. She was the Hulme brothers' mother, Marina. Whilst there, I also sensed someone staring at me. Someone else had recognised me. It was Herbert's mother, Christine. The night before she had served me as I grabbed some last minute shopping in Bacup's Co-op store. Now she recognised me in a different role as I transcribed shorthand notes from interviews I had carried out the previous day and wrote up stories from my notepad.

The court in session, Judge Anthony Russell went through with the barristers who was to be representing whom and each defendant was asked in turn how they pleaded, firstly to count

one of causing grievous bodily harm with intent to Rob Maltby. Each uttered two words: "Not guilty." Then the charge relating to Sophie Lancaster – that of murder, was put and again each responded again with: "Not guilty." As the case was proceeding, the silence of the courtroom was broken by a mobile phone going off in the public gallery. A relative of the accused chose to answer it. To my amazement he told the caller:

"I can't talk right now because I'm in court." He was reprimanded by Judge Russell.

It was announced that a pre-trial review would take place on February 22, 2008 with the trial date still March 10. The press was reminded that a Section 39 Order, which prohibited the identity of the accused being made public, was still in place. Harris and Herbert were again remanded in custody while the other three – the Hulme brothers and Mallett – remained on conditional bail. The case adjourned at 11.30am. As the trial was pending, I was instructed by my editor to keep reporting of stories relating to Sophie and the campaign to a minimum. He wanted to ensure that nothing written in the *Free Press* could be perceived as having an influence on potential jurors or be seen to prejudice the impending court proceedings.

From left to right:
Harris
Herbert
J Hulme
D Hulme
Mallet.

On February 22, 2008 the five once again appeared at Preston Crown Court, this time for a pre-trial review. My colleague Jenny Brookfield attended court. Judge Anthony Russell explained that the trial had been set for six weeks, two more that had previously been expected and the court was told there could be evidence heard from as many as 50 witnesses, many of whom would be present through a video link because of their age. All five defendants still denied the charges.

The judge ruled that legal representatives in the case would not be wearing their usual court attire of gowns and wigs due to the age of the witnesses involved. Judge Russell was also not going to be seen in his trademark red gown and wig, instead his chosen apparel would be a tailor-made pinstripe suit.

There was little free space inside the new courthouse. Each defendant had his own barrister with assistants and solicitors. The public gallery had to accommodate representatives from seven families, the five accused and two victims. Complaints were made that Sophie and Rob's families had to sit alongside relatives of the teenagers on trial. Judge Russell said the court would endeavour to make arrangements in future to seat them away from each other. Unfortunately, such was the interest in this case, it did not prove possible. At that hearing they sat with the press, but when the trial began there was not even enough room on the press bench to accommodate the media.

15

"Do you know anything about a press conference in Blackburn? I have been told I should really attend to put my side of what happened."

I was somewhat bemused when Sylvia announced this to me when she rang me at home. It was February and the trial was not due to start until March 10 so why would the police be arranging a press conference two weeks before? Previous murders I had covered had always led to a hastily arranged press conference after the trial, not before. I had to admit to her that it was not a move I had ever come across before.

My first call on the Monday morning was to Detective Inspector Holden who confirmed there was to be a press conference and that I would receive an invitation. He also explained that in 'high profile' cases police often arranged press conferences before to ensure all the facts and details of the case were already known, so that reporters would have their stories ready for the verdict. My only assumption was that the police were extremely confident that they had a watertight case and there was no way these teenagers were going to succeed with their 'not guilty' pleas. I spoke to Sylvia the day before the press conference. She was concerned that anything she said might have a bearing on the trial.

Monday February 25 was exactly two weeks before the trial

Superintendent Mick Gradwell and Detective Inspector Dean
Holden address the media at the press conference in February.

was due to start. After completing my usual tasks, I headed over
to Blackburn's new police base for the mid-afternoon confer-
ence. Apparently there was nowhere large enough in the
Pennine Division, which covers Rossendale, to host the event.
We all had to decamp to an industrial estate on the outskirts of
Blackburn, which is where the new headquarters is based.

Parking was difficult because the place was mobbed. I joined
the throng of journalists as a large media pack of newspaper,
radio, TV and internet reporters, photographers and camera-
men gathered in the station's large foyer. Many had heard of the
case but knew little of the fine detail. We all filed through the
rabbit warren of a building and into a conference room. At the
back, a sea of video and TV cameras lined up like an army of
soldiers. Print media occupied around 30 seats and I found myself sitting next to a former newspaper colleague turned radio
journalist, David Saville. Before the conference began, every

journalist had to sign in, log an email contact address and agree that no information mentioned at the hearing would be used until the conclusion of the trial. Everyone wanted the details, so all agreed to these conditions.

Superintendent Mick Gradwell and Detective Inspector Dean Holden were sitting behind a small table in front of a police backdrop. The Detective Inspector was a shadow of his much larger colleague and he opened the conference by outlining the background to the case. He recounted the events of that night and the subsequent police investigation leading to that all-important trial we were all waiting for. It was clear that these hardened reporters, with their many years experience of horrific crimes, were shocked at the severity of what had transpired that night in the park. They struggled to contain their composure as Detective Inspector Holden in his softly spoken voice recounted with graphic detail what happened. They audibly took in gasps of breath and muttered about how they couldn't believe this girl had been killed just because she was a Goth, merely because of how she looked.

"Rob has been previously targeted because of the way he dresses," the detective told the assembled reporters.

He explained how the couple had left their friend's house and headed to the service station on Market Street. There they met some teenagers and eventually ended up in Stubbylee Park.

"From speaking to witnesses, he was attacked because he was a Mosher. One person was heard to say, 'He is a Mosher; hit him.' He was hit once by one offender and remained standing. Then he let out a laugh, we think it was a nervous laugh. Rob offered no retaliation. Rob and Sophie were not confrontational, but as a result of Rob's response, other comments were made among the group of five. 'He's laughing,' one said. 'You can't let him get away with it,' said another.

"The five then beat him to the floor, stamping and kicking him about the head rendering him unconscious. Sophie went to his aid and she shouted for them to stop. There was a break in the assault and Sophie knelt down at the side of Rob and was cradling his head in her lap. One or two then kicked her to the floor.

"She was subject to a very brutal attack. They stamped and kicked her about the head and there was very little, or no, opportunity for her to protect herself or retaliate."

He went on to describe the emergency calls and the couple's ambulance transfers to hospital. The detective described the behaviour of the five youths as 'feral'.

"It was so senseless. There was no reason behind it; the couple offered no threat. They were not responsible for the attack."

He described how both Sophie and Rob's faces bore footwear impressions of the laces and soles of the trainers that had been the implements used to attack them.

"This was most horrendous crime I have seen in 14 years as a police officer."

The detective praised key witnesses in the park at the time who gave evidence to the police. They also followed the instructions of the ambulance personnel and administered first aid to Sophie and Rob.

"The young people did their best for Sophie and Rob. Their action has to be praised. Those witnesses also provided the key evidence to the police – names of those responsible."

He described Herbert as the 'primary offender' but could not say clearly who had made that first comment, 'Let's get them'. Once the detective had finished his statement, he answered the many questions fielded by journalists, some of whom were encountering the story for the first time. As I had been in constant contact with the detective since the incident, and he was aware that I was very familiar with the location, when some questions were posed that he was not sure of the answer, he asked me to assist with locations. His boss, Superintendent Mick Gradwell, took over and criticised the attitude of the accused and their relatives when the police were questioning their sons. He told how Harris's mum Martine McGuinn had been laughing with her son as he was arrested for murder. He spoke of how the Hulme brothers' father gave his lads a false alibi saying his sons had been in Manchester all night when the attack had taken place. He was threatened with being arrested and charged with attempting to pervert the course of justice. He also said that the Hulme's father had made comments to belittle an officer who had asked one of his sons to look up when he was being asked a question.

"They didn't care about anything. They were just not bothered. To them the only thing they did wrong was to get caught. The fact that kids this age were let out between 1am and 2am shows an almost total lack of parental responsibility. I am very critical of the parents' attitudes both during the arrests and subsequent interviews and in letting their children go out and do what they want."

The questioning over, there was a short recess as the reporters awaited the arrival of Sylvia. Contrary to her comments to me the previous day, she had decided to address the media. She was wearing Sophie's gothic pendant cross around her neck and a trademark black 'S.O.P.H.I.E.' band on her arm. There were numerous cameras focused on that small table, reporters with their pens poised on notebooks ready to copy down her every word and several microphones positioned in front of her. It was a daunting sight for anyone, but for someone who had never been in the media spotlight before it must have been terrifying. Without doubt, Sylvia was the one they were all there to hear.

She was the one they wanted to quote. She was the person who had kept out of the spotlight and away from public scrutiny, so far. When she did deliver her well-prepared statement she was very controlled in her comments; never letting her guard down, at least not in public. She never outwardly condemned or chastised those responsible for her daughter's death. Her words were measured, yet descriptive and well thought out. It was insightful and it painted a picture of the girl who was now just that, a photograph and a memory.

Full credit to the journalists. They didn't try to trick or persuade Sylvia to say things she might regret. They were very respectful of her situation. Sylvia explained that Sophie and Rob had met through a mutual friend. Rob had attended the same school where Joseph Hulme had been a student, Bacup and Rawtenstall Grammar School while Sophie went to Haslingden High School.

"You could try to contain her but it didn't work. She liked reading, read a lot, was very bright and intelligent. When I talk about Sophie it is very difficult. She was just coming into her own, finding her self-confidence. She wanted to do youth work and she had an interest in journalism because of the writing aspect."

She explained how what had happened had an effect on her own work with young offenders through Connexions, an agency for young people aged 13–19 who want advice on how to get on in life. It also provides support up to the age of 25 for young people who have learning difficulties or disabilities and works with a variety of agencies.

"The difference is I have always been a lefty Liberal, but now I come from the other side; this is how it is and I think that can only help. I haven't lost my faith." When she said: "I know her individuality could make her a target," her comment was picked up by a female journalist who asked: "Did you never ask your daughter to change her appearance so she might not have faced the prejudice shown to her that night?"

Sylvia replied: "Why would I ask her to change what she was?"

She said the last six months was like being in *Alice Through the Looking Glass*; none of it seemed real. It was bizarre. She took the opportunity to explain how the family had launched the S.O.P.H.I.E. campaign and that workshops would be held with youth groups in the valley to teach tolerance of different subcultures. She explained how many people had used cyber-space to tell of their own experience at the hands of intolerant people who thought nothing of hitting and striking someone because they were dressed differently. Asked what she missed most about her daughter, Sylvia said:

"I miss her presence and her laughter because she had quite a sense of humour."

She told the journalists she understood that, from talking to Rob since the attack, the couple would probably have married. Asked for her abiding memory, she talked of Sophie's smile.

"She was like a little doll, a porcelain doll – that reflects how she was on the inside. She was kind and very caring."

Sylvia then left the room. She had held it together remark-ably well. The assembled media were given the chance to have one-to-one interviews with the senior police officers, but not Sylvia. These were carried out in various locations throughout the busy police station and as I had a couple of questions of my own that I wished clearing up, I joined the queue to put my questions face-to-face to Detective Inspector Holden.

"If those teenagers had not made those phone calls from the park while the attack was taking place, do you think we could have been looking at a double murder?"

"Yes, we probably would have," he replied.

16

There was a strong prosecution case against all five. Surely the weight of evidence was going to make them realise they had been caught in the act and would admit to their actions. Police found forensic evidence of blood on Herbert's trousers. It was also on his socks and his shoes and it was not only traced to Rob, but also to Sophie. Herbert's top had been washed before his arrest.

The trial was set to begin and colleagues pleaded with the editor to allow the case to be covered properly, by attending court every day and not relying on press agencies. He agreed. On that first day, Monday March 10, 2008, I joined the queue waiting to go through the security checks. There was already a crowd from various media starting to assemble outside court. The telltale white vans with huge satellite dishes could be seen on a side road. Cameras set up on tripods were clicking away capturing images of all who attended court for whatever reason. They were desperate to capture an image of those boys on bail. They were also seeking the families of Sophie and Rob, and if possible Rob himself.

That first day at court was not expected to be a long one. The trial was due to open, hear pleas and then adjourn for a jury to be sworn in. They were all down to plead not guilty – surely the day's proceedings wouldn't last very long. I stupidly only paid for three hours on the car park. Justice is never predictable and always works to its own timetable.

I didn't want to miss grabbing a seat on the press bench. A Lancashire Police press officer handed the media a copy of prosecutor Michael Shorrock's opening address. Here we had an outline of the case set to be delivered once we were finally allowed into the courtroom. With one eye on the door, should anything start happening, I began masking out a story using the prosecution notes as my guide. Then the press officer announced nothing would be happening until after lunch, at least 2pm. The pay and display parking ticket on my car was set to expire so I left court to renew it. Had I not had friends among the media pack that could have been the most expensive parking ticket of my journalistic career. As I was putting more pounds in the meter, the court hastily resumed at 12.55pm and Herbert's guilty plea to both counts was accepted. On returning to the cafe within the court building I could not believe the bombshell dropped on me.

"He has done what? Oh shit, I don't believe I've missed it."

On my mobile there was a text message from a friend in Bacup asking which one of them had pleaded – it had already been on the national news. Fortunately, a colleague had been in court and noted down exactly what had been said. Richard Marks QC, defending Herbert, told the court he had received a report that morning and, as a consequence of the conversation with a psychiatrist and a psychologist, there was no 'live defence' available.

"He accepts responsibility for the attack on both victims."

Herbert was remanded in custody for a pre-sentence report.

As he was taken down, Judge Anthony Russell warned him:

"The sentence of the court is fixed at life, it is a question of the minimum term."

At that stage Herbert could not be identified. When the court finally resumed that afternoon just four young men were standing in the dock – Mallett, the Hulme brothers and Harris. It was a packed courtroom. The small press bench quickly filled up and other reporters found themselves sitting on the vacant jury seats. Family members of the victims and the accused were seated side-by-side in the small public gallery to the left of the press benches. As the charge of causing grievous bodily harm with intent on Rob was put to each of them, first Harris, then Joseph Hulme, Danny Hulme and Mallett all uttered the one word response of: "Guilty."

Then came the sting in the tail as prosecuting barrister Mr Shorrock rose to his feet.

"All four defendants have pleaded not guilty on the first count of the murder of Sophie Lancaster. I have considered very carefully what the position is now. Having regard to the evidence in this case, my conclusion will have to be a trial in so far as Harris is concerned. There is direct evidence of his involvement in the killing of Sophie Lancaster. There is direct evidence from witnesses. The bulk of evidence tends to show the attack started on Rob Maltby and only moved on to Sophie Lancaster at a later stage."

In the original prosecution opening, distributed to the press before Herbert changed his plea, counsel was proposing to hold them all accountable on the grounds that they participated in a 'joint enterprise'. The justification was that if two or more persons agree to commit a crime and set about carrying out that crime, then each is as guilty of that crime even though they may

play completely different parts. This changed when the pleas of guilty to the offence against Rob were accepted.

"There is no direct evidence either of the Hulme brothers or Mallett encouraging them [Herbert and Harris] to attack Sophie. That being so, we are minded to offer no evidence against them on that count. There is no direct evidence of any actual assault on Sophie Lancaster by Mallett, or Danny Hulme."

There was forensic evidence implicating Danny Hulme in Rob's attack because Rob's blood was found on the upper front and tongue of his training shoe. The court heard this supported the accusation that he was present and close to Rob at the time he was bleeding or being assaulted. Regarding Joseph Hulme, Mr Shorrock said one witness had said it was either him or Harris he saw kicking Sophie.

"We think, over all, justice is done by offering no evidence."

Judge Anthony Russell ruled:

"I fully understand why the crown has adopted this position. It seems to me, in light of what you have said, it is the appropriate course; with offering no evidence I record a verdict of not guilty."

This meant that four people involved in the attack that night, Herbert, Mallett and the Hulme brothers would not appear in the witness box. Their version of events would not be heard and the families of Sophie and Rob would never have the chance to see and hear them cross-examined by the prosecution.

The judge's adjudication over, it was then the turn for defence counsel to plead with Judge Russell to allow their clients, Mallett and the Hulme brothers, to remain on bail. Paul Reid QC, for Joseph Hulme, said: "He is coming to the end of a course at Myerscough College. If he completes the next three to four weeks then this year will not have been wasted." A plea for Mallett was made by David Fish QC who spoke of his client's Crohn's Disease and psoriasis and him needing to attend a hospital appointment in Burnley at the end of the month. Judge Russell's response was quick and swift. He immediately remanded the four to join Herbert in custody. As they were taken down, one defendant shouted to his mother:

"Love you, mum."

The comment was later condemned by Judge Russell when passing sentence, as was the wink one of the defendants exchanged with the public gallery when it became clear they were no longer standing trial for murder. Sylvia Lancaster would never again hear her daughter say that she loved her.

17

After a day of legal arguments and the swearing in of the jury of nine men and three women, the trial of Harris got under-way on Wednesday March 12, 2008. Another set of opening statements had been prepared and could finally be delivered by prosecutor Michael Shorrock QC. The ensuing courtroom drama spread over three weeks. It saw jury members in tears as the graphic evidence of what transpired was revealed.

Mr Shorrock said: "The attack was totally unprovoked. It would appear that Mr Maltby and Miss Lancaster were singled out, not for anything that they had said or done, but because they looked and dressed differently to the defendant and his friends. When on the ground, kicks rained in to his [Rob's] head and body. His head was jumped and stamped on. He made no attempt to defend himself. He was rendered unconscious.

"The reason for the attack on Rob Maltby appears to have been simply because he looked and dressed differently to them. He was, what they described as, a Goth or a Mosher."

As so often happens in cases like this, counsel have to use words which are not in their routine vocabulary. Mr Shorrock's pronunciation of the word Mosher for some reason became, 'Mowsher'. Mr Shorrock told how a 14-year-old girl had given a statement to police saying she saw Harris jump up and kick

Rob in the head. The girl told police Herbert, known to the local youths as Peanut, punched Rob and he went to the floor.

"Then according to this witness they all started kicking him. She describes how the defendants were 'right near' Rob Maltby encouraging each other and laughing. At this stage that young girl ran away and left the scene."

Another 14-year-old girl told the police all five defendants had been at the skate ramps and she said Herbert, Joe Hulme and Harris had said they should 'start on them'[Sophie and Rob] while others had said the couple were being nice to everyone. She too confirmed Harris struck Rob first and echoed the first witness's description of Rob laughing and the others shouting out when he did.

"I definitely saw Joe Hulme, Harris and Herbert hitting him. Harris hit him in the face; Joe Hulme was kicking him. Herbert was bending over him and punching him in the face. All five were having a go. All five were round him. Sophie was trying to push them off."

Another witness told how Sophie and Rob had been posing for a photograph just before the attack happened. But while the photo was being taken, she heard a gang of youths decide to attack the pair. The court was shown two police interviews with a 15-year-old girl who was in the park at the time. In the first she did not say she had witnessed the start of the attack, but in the second interview she admitted she had been there but said she was concerned that she may be the only witness to come forward. She told police she had met Sophie and they had gone into the skate park together. She described hearing someone say: "Oh let's start on him."

In a recorded police interview a witness, who was 16 at the time, described how he saw Herbert hitting Rob. He said Herbert grabbed him and then asked if Rob wanted an ambulance. When Rob replied 'no', the witness said Herbert hit him again. The attack left the Manchester art student with 22 separate injuries. Many were as a result of direct kicks to his head, which rendered him unconscious, bleeding and in a coma. His girlfriend's pleas for them to stop and leave her boyfriend alone fell on deaf ears.

A 17-year-old boy, who gave evidence in court via a video link, described how the rest of the group joined in the attack saying he didn't see any reason why it had begun.

"I saw him [Harris] swing for the lad [Rob], he went to hit him. Then I could just see arms flying and legs raised everywhere. It was one big group. He was just on the floor helpless. He was getting kicked and punched. I ran over and tried to stop it. I shouted at them to stop and pushed him [Harris] away. I told them to leave him alone."

The teenager told how Sophie was covering Rob to stop him being hit.

"She was shouting, 'Stop, leave him alone,' and trying to protect him. She was kneeling down over him."

He left the park with friends, saying Sophie was 'perfectly fine' when he departed. Mr Shorrock said Harris and Herbert then turned their attention on Sophie. Not wanting to leave such a key witness to their unprovoked attack, Herbert and Harris took it upon themselves to kick and stamp her life out.

A 16-year-old boy told police: "I think she had his head on her lap and they were all stood around, not moving anywhere and Brendan [Harris] kicked the girl. And then I left the scene for about five minutes and when I went back to the skate ramps she was on the floor then."

While he was away, the petite size eight gap-year student was horrifically injured and 13 days later those injuries were to prove fatal.

The 16-year-old went on to explain how he, and two others, left the skate ramps and went to the Fudge Factory and phoned an ambulance. On returning to the skate park they found both Sophie and Rob bleeding and unconscious.

A 15-year-old witness told how he heard someone shout 'hit him' before the attack on Rob began.

"I don't know exactly who punched him, but I'm sure it was them five [Harris, Herbert, Mallett and the Hulme brothers] who hit the guy." A short time later, when this witness returned to the skate ramps, he saw Herbert and Harris kicking Sophie in the head. His statement said she was already on the floor.

"It looked like they were running over and just like kicking her in the head and jumping up and down on her head or summat … they were kicking her all over her head."

A 14-year-old girl told police how there was a big group on the skate park including the five and the two people she described as 'Moshers' – Sophie and Rob.

"They were just talking, being all right with everyone, just talking normally to everyone." She left the area but on her return she described seeing Rob on the floor and Sophie sitting next to him trying to help him.

"I started crying because I'd never seen anything like that. They were all just booting him."

She described how a friend pleaded with the gang to leave Rob alone, but they ignored him.

The jury heard from Sophie and Rob's friend Jonathan Smethurst, who had spent the night with the couple before they went off to the park.

A statement was read out from Rob, which said he had no recollection of the incident. In fact, he had no knowledge of what transpired from 24 hours prior to the attack until he was woken from his coma in hospital.

"When I was in hospital I was told Sophie was in hospital as well. My mum came in and told me that there was little chance they could save her. The last time that I saw Sophie was on the Wednesday. I went to hospital and saw her on the intensive care ward. It has been posted around the papers that we were attacked because we were Goths but we really weren't. The only difference was I had long hair and Sophie had dreadlocks. We were just individual, didn't have a name for it. Usually when me and Sophie met a large group we would normally speak to their girlfriends because they were normally nicer to us. When we met people that weren't like us, they would normally ask Sophie about her piercings."

He documented an earlier assault when the couple had been out to celebrate Sophie's birthday the previous November. He told how they were in Rochdale when he was attacked and struck on the head. His statement concluded that he felt he was more likely to be attacked because of how he dressed and how he looked.

18

On the first day of Harris's trial, the jury heard the emergency calls made by the youngsters who had witnessed the attack. Those three calls were made by terrified teens on their mobile phones, desperate to get help for these two 'Moshers'.

As the attack happened, a 14-year-old girl called the emergency services in spite of the potential harm that could befall her. Her terrified voice rang out in court and all present listened for 14 minutes as the girl described the horrific scene. Her fear was audible. Every juror, member of the public, press, counsel and the Judge could not fail to be moved by the account of what she was describing – the attack was still happening when she made the call. The families of Sophie and Rob were too distressed to stay and here the tape of their loved ones being attacked and their injuries described in graphic detail; Sylvia left the court in tears. The child's voice screamed down the phone in a hysterical state. When the tape finished, the girl, who was being interviewed by video link, was sobbing uncontrollably and crying out for her mum. Judge Russell ruled she was in no fit state to continue and adjourned proceedings.

*

Bacup is a very close-knit community and when people discovered that calls had been made to the emergency services, the youngsters who tried to help were criticised by some for not alerting the police and ambulance sooner. Sylvia too cannot comprehend that the teenagers left the scene before making that first call for help and she disputes the notion that their actions were 'brave'. She questioned why they did not try to stop the initial attack on Rob or alert the authorities from inside the park while it was happening; maybe then her daughter would never have been set upon.

Three calls were made to the ambulance service that night, the first at 1.17am. I was not in court when these calls were brought into evidence, but after reading, and rereading the transcripts, I couldn't help wondering if the emergency services had been sent in the wrong direction – to Waterfoot, just over a mile away towards Rawtenstall. The second call, the girl's, lasted 14 minutes. Only at the end of that call, at around 1.32am, can the girl be heard to say the ambulance has arrived in Stubbylee Park. Why Waterfoot? Well, on four separate occasions in the controller's conversation with the lad who makes the first and third calls, he is asked if he is in Bacup or Waterfoot – why when the youngsters only talk about being in Bacup?

When you want to quiz authorities, it is no longer a case of just asking the question. Paramedics have not been allowed to speak directly to the press for many years, gone are the days when reporters could find out people's names, ages and addresses and why an ambulance was called to a specific address or location.

After explaining my concerns to Sylvia, I asked if she was all right with me making a Freedom of Information request to the ambulance service to try to get an answer to the missing minutes. She agreed and the letter was sent on May 25, 2009. The North West Ambulance Service responded on June 1 to say that there may be a charge for the information requested. Then, in a further letter dated June 4, it wrote: 'Since there are issues of patient confidentiality that are involved in answering your questions, I should be pleased if you could confirm your status (eg next of kin etc) with regard to your request. If you are not acting in any capacity of this nature, the Trust will require the written consent of the patient (or if appropriate next of kin etc) before information can be released to you.'

Sylvia immediately forwarded a letter giving approval for the questions to be answered. In less than a month the reply came, dated June 23, it stated that the ambulance had gone to Bacup, not to Waterfoot. There was still no justification for the delay in it arriving at the park. After discussing the letter's contents with Sylvia, it was decided to probe further where the crew went. The first response prompted more questions than it provided answers. We wanted to know why it took so long for the ambulance to arrive at the park when, in their written response, the service said it despatched the first ambulance at 1.18 am and from Stacksteads Ambulance Station, a mile away from the park. Together, on June 25, we composed a further letter asking more questions. We mistakenly thought we might finally get an answer to the missing minutes – how wrong we were.

It must be hard to be an ambulance controller based far away from a scene, with no local knowledge, and dealing with a hysterical and terrified teenage girl who was, at times, screaming down the telephone. The 15-year-old boy was more composed in his two calls, making the first at 1.17 am. In his statement he said he had made the call from Park Road. He had left Stubbylee and the skate park and had wandered back to the place where the group had originally congregated. He crucially only mentioned the attack on Rob; he never said there was a second victim. That first call lasted two minutes.

The 14-year-old girl called for help from the skate park at 1.19 am. While she was talking to the controller, the 15-year-old boy dialled 999 again, this time it was logged at 1.23 am. The boy's initial call described the location as 'Bacup Park, near Bacup, Bacup Park, Park Road'. The controller asks: "And you're definitely on Park Road?"

"Yeah, Park Road, you go up, turn in and there's Bacup Park and there's a lad just been battered."

Had that ambulance arrived more quickly, it is almost certain that its crew would have witnessed the incident taking place and would have been able to administer first aid to the victims sooner. However they could also have been placing themselves in jeopardy. During those intervening minutes, two ambulance controllers gave detailed instructions to the three teenagers who remained in the park that night on how to administer first aid and how to try to stem the flow of blood which was pouring from the serious head wounds the couple had received.

The proper name for the park is in fact Stubbylee Park not Bacup Park, and it is not in Park Road, it is in New Line. Three pages into the girl's call she says:

"Everyone still on him but don't tell 'em I'm on the phone to you, right."

Although she has called for help, she is also terrified in case her 'friends', who are carrying out the attack, realise what she has done. While she is speaking, a male voice can be heard saying: "Oi, get the fuck off him now."

Something is clearly still taking place at the time of this call, according to the 'him' reference. Is it an attack on Rob or is it the attack on Sophie or was it really 'get off them'?

Then the girl walks past Sophie and Rob and a male voice can be heard saying: "What you doing?" Is this directed at the girl who is following instructions of the ambulance controller to try to find out how Rob is? Only when reading the end of the fourth page does the girl mention that Sophie – dubbed 'his bird' – is also on the floor; not that she is being attacked, but that Sophie has already been injured. She too is asked for a location and says: "In Bacup Park, on the skate ramp, Bacup Park." When quizzed further the girl says: "Erm, its on Park Road, at Bacup, it's called Stubbylee Park." The controller repeats Park Road and says she knows Park Road but again queries the name of the park.

"Stubbylee Park, Park Road, Stubbylee Park on the skate ramp on the park."

The message relayed from the ambulance controller to the police was: "Assault in a park, Park Road, possibly near a skate park." This was deemed serious enough for the call for a response to be sent out to two police sergeants and three patrol cars. The first place they checked was Edgeside Park in Waterfoot, arriving at 1.34 am. Edgeside Park is on Park Road and has a skate park. Why would the ambulance controller give different messages to the police and paramedics? If the police interpreted that log to mean Waterfoot, why would the ambulance respond differently? At no time in any of the three phone calls do the teenagers mention Waterfoot and yet half way through the transcript of the second conversation with the 15-year-old boy the controller curiously asks: "Right, Stubbylee Park is that actually in Bacup itself?" The boy replies: "Er yeah." And the controller says: "It's not in Waterfoot, is it?"

That was the reason I became convinced that the ambulance

had been sent the wrong way. The controller goes on to question the boy as to whether he is in Waterfoot or Bacup a further three times with the final statement: "Right, that, are we definitely in, we're definitely in Bacup and we're definitely not in Waterfoot?" This comes on page 11 of the 12-page transcript.

These children pleaded over and over for the emergency crews to come quickly because 'they're dying'. They were brave to make those calls. They did indeed plead for help while the attack/s were still taking place. They knew just what their friends were capable of, they had just witnessed it, yet they still had the courage to ring for help. In desperation they pleaded with the ambulance to hurry up. Following instructions they removed their clothing to try to stop the flow of blood from Sophie and Rob.

Why did it take so long for paramedics to arrive at the scene? In the early hours of the morning, it could reasonably be expected that the vehicle may have been on another call-out and so another station might have dealt with the emergency, but it wasn't. The ambulance was sent from Stacksteads. It is just over a minute away under blues and twos. Traffic on the main Newchurch Road, which runs through the valley bottom, would have been very light in the early hours of a Saturday morning. The ambulance crews would probably have to face a handful of taxis delivering night-time revellers back home and that would be about it. What was the delay? I travelled the distance myself, late at night, and even at 30mph I made the park in Waterfoot in two-and-a-half minutes while it took just two minutes to arrive at Stubbylee Park. Had I been travelling for 14 minutes – the time it took the ambulance to arrive, then I would have travelled nearly seven miles, an ambulance with its lights and sirens would obviously have gone much further.

★

The trust responded to our call for further clarification by ringing me to query whether our inquiries could lead to legal action but, understandably, Sylvia said:

"I have no idea until I know what the answers are."

I relayed Sylvia's answer to the trust's Patient Advice and Liaison Services manager and they agreed the legal services manager should review the queries in case there was any subsequent legal action. On August 24 I received a further letter asking again for written consent from Sylvia, which she again provided. Then in late September when I had still not received a reply I rang and asked why I was still waiting for a response, only to be told they had not received Sylvia's letter. So once again another letter, the third Sylvia had to write, was despatched and our wait went on.

Finally, on November 4, I received a letter from the North West Ambulance Service. At last, I thought, the answer to my queries – no such luck. They apologised for the delay and then proceeded to reply to my first set of questions and give different answers. The follow-up letter says the first call was made at 1.18 am and the third at 1.25 am. The initial letter stated the first call was received at 1.17 am and the third at 1.23 am. The second letter said the first ambulance became mobile at 1.19 am, but the first letter said that the ambulance was despatched at 1.18 am. To date, I have not received an answer to the second questions posed not just by me, but also by Sylvia too. The North West Ambulance Service said it would not respond until we could clarify if some legal action would follow. We have given them the only answer possible at this stage. We just wanted to get to the truth and find out what happened that night.

The following are excerpts from the transcripts of all three conversations with ambulance controllers. Throughout the early part of the phone calls male voices can be heard in the background – the attacks are clearly still taking place.

According to information supplied by the ambulance service to the initial letter, the first call, at 1.17am, is from a 15-year-old boy – this is the only call made away from the scene. He explains the location as Bacup Park, and says that a lad has been 'battered'. The controller queries which town and he says: "Bacup Park, please, quick, it's urgent."

"Yeah, well you have to slow down, I'm in a control room."

He says he can't hear the controller and is again asked for the address.

"Bacup Park near Bacup, Bacup Park, Park Road."

"Park Road?"

"Yeah, Bacup Park."

"And you're definitely on Park Road?"

"Yeah, Park Road, you go up, turn in and there's Bacup Park and there's a lad just been battered."

The call ends and the controller asks the operator to confirm that the lad has cleared the line. Then comes the call from a terrified 14-year-old girl, a recording of which was issued to members of the press following her court appearance. Her hysterical voice was heard on TV, radio and posted on news websites. From her comments, and the noises in the background of the tape, she is clearly at the scene when this call is made and the attack is still ongoing; the time is 1.19am.

"We need, we need an ambulance at Bacup Park, this Mosher's just been banged because he's a Mosher, we need an ambulance at Bacup Park quick on the skate park."

Her sobs can be heard and the controller asks her to calm down.

"This poor guy, I don't even know him, and I'm crying me eyes out, I don't even know him."

Again, she is asked to calm down.

"I think he's dead."

When the witness calms enough to try to give a more precise location, she says Bacup Park, on the skate ramp, Bacup Park.

"Erm, it's on Park Road at Bacup, it's called Stubbylee Park."

"Park Road."

"Park Road, Stubbylee Park, right; it's a Mosher just been banged for no reason."

"Right I know Park Road, what actual park are you on?"

The girl repeats Stubbylee Park and then she again says Stubbylee Park, Park Road, on the skate ramp.

"Yeah we need an ambulance quick cos he's lying on the floor, he's not even breathing."

In the background male voices can be heard. One says: "Get the fuck off him now please."

"But I don't even know him, but he's just been battered, and it's horrible." Again a male voice can be heard in the background of the call saying: "Oi get the fuck off him now."

"Everyone's still on him, but don't tell 'em I'm on the phone to you, right." Someone can be heard saying: "Get off him, now."

The terrified girl warns the controller if she goes quiet she is walking past them. She bravely then goes up to the scene and a sinister male voice asks: "What you doing?"

In the background other voices can be heard although their speech is inaudible. A male can be heard saying: "What you standing about, he's on the floor man, he's practically fucking dead kicking his head in."

Responding to questions, the girl tells the controller Rob is about 20. Then a male voice calls to her to leave the scene. The controller asks if Rob is conscious and the girl responds: "I, only I can't, I can't get him, cos they'll all get, I don't know."

Another male voice can be heard in the background and then for the first time the caller mentions Sophie, on the fourth of 19 pages in the transcript.

"Just let me go and see if he's conscious. I'm not leaving, conscious or not, see if he's conscious, his bird's on the floor as well."

"His what?"

"His bird's on the floor as well."

Another male voice can be heard saying: "... cos you're fucking pathetic." The gang are obviously still in the park.

The controller quizzes whether by 'bird' she means his girlfriend.

"Yeah, his girlfriend's on the floor as well. They're still breathing but they're full of blood, please send an ambulance quick."

Then her hysterical voice says she can't touch Rob because he's full of blood.

"Right, listen to me, I need to know if he's unconscious or not."

The 15-year-old boy makes his second call to the emergency services at 1.23am and he describes blood pouring from the couple's heads. He can be heard talking to another ambulance controller in the background of the girl's call. When asked if the couple have both been assaulted the girl replies: "Yeah, both of them, cos they're Moshers."

She realises her friend has also used his phone to report the incident.

"Please, my friend's on the phone to them now, I'm not going

Skate park.

to get done for reporting this, am I? Because all the Bacup lot'll hate me because I've reported it."

The controller again calms the caller down and asks who is there with her and she explains that two other boys are present. She tells the girl to take some deep breaths and then she can try to help Sophie and Rob, all the time asking her to find out if the couple are still breathing. The girl describes Sophie and Rob making 'stupid noises' like they can't breathe. The controller asks if the attackers are still there.

"No, cos they ran when we were walking down, cos we wondered what had happened."

She says she didn't see what happened. The girl is given instructions on how to stop the bleeding. She removes her T-shirt and puts her jacket back on and instructs the two boys, who are still with her at the skate park, to remove their T-shirts to try to suppress the bleeding by following instructions and pushing down on the wounds. But when the girl explains that both Sophie and Rob are bleeding all over their heads she is instructed to put the T-shirt on top of the head.

"Oi, put the T-shirt where they're bleeding, put the T-shirt where they're bleeding, put the T-shirt where they're bleeding. (shrieking) Oh I can't, I can't do it, where is the ambulance, please."

She explains that the boys are following her instructions. The controller asks if the bleeding is coming through the T-shirts.

"No, it's all over their hands, all coming out of their eyes, out their nose and everything, please just help us quick, please, please."

When Rob starts to convulse, the girl is told to place him on his side and she instructs the boys to put both Rob and Sophie in the recovery position. As she waits for the ambulance one of the most harrowing statements is made:

"They're horrible, they can't hear, they're just laid there with blood all over their face, they can't even move, they just look like dummies."

The controller establishes that the second caller is one of the boys helping the girl and she breaks down in tears. She is crying as she talks about her friend.

"Yeah, he's worried as well. Oh I've never seen anyone like this before, it's horrible."

Then the girl can be heard talking to Sophie or Rob saying: "Stay where you are, the ambulance is on it's way, pal, just stay where you are, it's coming for you, it's going to help ya, come on now."

She is asked to check if Sophie is still breathing and the witness describes seeing her belly moving.

"That's the only thing, that's the only I can do, cos that, that much blood really."

She is quizzed about Rob.

"He, he's just laid on floor, his head's on the floor."

She describes seeing a big group running off from the park 'loads of people' but does not say how many. As the ambulance arrives the girl begins to have a panic attack and says she too is struggling for breath. The controller talks her through what is happening to her and calms the girl.

"Just take some deep breaths please, it'll help you. In through your nose and out through your mouth, just calm down."

The ambulance crew arrive. The girl adds that she was just walking through the park when she saw lots of people run off. The controller ends the conversation.

When the 15-year-old calls back at 1.23 am he pleads: "Please, they're fucking dying, please, please."

He is again quizzed about the location and he says Park Road, Stubbylee Park, Bacup.

"What's the problem?"

"There's two people been battered, there's blood coming out their heads and they can't breathe properly, and then, oh, you have to ring back, I don't think one can breathe properly."

He describes blood coming out of Sophie's head and he is given advice to stem the flow of blood by removing his T-shirt, folding it into a pad and pressing it to the wound. Before he gets chance to do so he says he thinks one has stopped breathing and is given instructions to put the injured person flat on their back. The controller explains how to adjust their head to help with breathing.

"Right okay, right, put your ear next to their mouth and see if you feel or hear any breathing or …"

"He's bleeding, he's bleeding, it's just coming out of him."

He is asked if he is breathing.

"No there's blood out of his nose, his eyes, the side of his head, the mouth." He is told to wrap his T-shirt around Rob's head.

"At least you're going to try and stop the bleeding, all right."

He says he can't see where the blood is coming from and the controller tells him to get his girlfriend to hold the T-shirt in place.

"The girl, no his girlfriend is knocked out and all. She's got blood coming out of her head."

He explains there are three of them in the park trying to help 'but they're panicking really bad'. He is instructed to get them to help.

"One of 'em, the lad's woke up now. He's putting his head up, oh pal, pal. Pal can you hear me, can you hear me, can you hear me, oi talk to me."

In the background groaning and gurgling noises can be heard. It is clearly Rob. The controller asks about weapons.

"I don't know, we just found 'em up park, but can you hear me?"

The boy talks to Rob, asking him to say something. The boy tells the controller that Sophie is not breathing.

"Will you please come with an ambulance, we don't know what to do."

"Listen to me, are you in Waterfoot or are you in Bacup itself?"

"We're in Bacup."

"You're in Bacup?"

"On the park, right, will you just please come? We need some help now."

He is told the ambulance is coming. The controller asks about Sophie's condition and asks him to try to get her to calm down.

She believes the female voice in the background is Sophie, but it is actually the teenage girl who is also on the phone to the ambulance service and is talking in a hysterical voice.

"She, she, she can't. She's not hearing me. She's not breathing. She's knocked out."

The controller then advises him to lie Sophie flat on her back with nothing under her head and tilt her head.

"Will you get here, please."

"Listen, we're coming as fast as we can."

"There's blood coming out of her ears and now her eyes, there's blood coming out of her eyes and her ears."

He is then advised to put a T-shirt around Sophie's head to stem the flow of blood.

"How long is this ambulance gonna be?"

"Help is already being sent and we're sending the police up as well, all right, but I need you to help these people in the meantime."

The boy explains that Sophie is breathing 'a little bit'. There is a discussion about the girl who is also talking to the ambulance service. Then the controller says: "Now just let me check, you're definitely not in, are you in Waterfoot or not?"

"Er, the lad's getting up, are you all right pal, oi pal you've gotta get with your girlfriend, your girlfriend's proper bad, come on pal."

The girl can be heard in the background saying to Rob to stay where he is and the ambulance is on its way. The controller advises the boy to leave Rob because he is not in a fit state to help his girlfriend.

"Right, that, are we definitely in, we're definitely in Bacup and we're definitely not in Waterfoot?" Then the lad says Rob's belly is not moving. The controller asks if he is breathing and the boy is asked to check for a pulse. The boy is told to lay Rob flat and put his ear against Rob's mouth to feel or hear him breathing and to put his hand on his chest to feel if it rises.

"Yeah, I can feel some, feel sommat moving."

The ambulance arrives, the call ends.

★

Giving evidence in court, one witness said one of the defendants said: "We'll bang them."

The boy told the jury: "I said to him, 'No we won't. No one's going to touch them.' They had both been really nice."

He said he saw Harris and Herbert attacking Sophie.

"They were the only ones I seen. They were running over and just kicking her in the head and jumping up and down on their heads. When I seen it happening I ran over. I'm not just going to stand there and watch am I and let someone get kicked in the head?"

Harrowing. It was the one-word headline the *Free Press* used on the front-page of March 14. This was the first time the newspaper had been able to put into print any of the trial information, which had been published nationally since the case began on the Monday. The paper's website had been kept updated since the start of the court hearing in Preston when Herbert changed his plea. The coverage instantly became the site's most viewed page. The front page recounted the chilling 999 call made by the 14-year-old girl.

19

Photographs of the facial injuries suffered by Sophie and Rob were shown to the Judge, jury and counsel. These pictures, taken 44 hours after the attack, were eventually released to the press after the trial and have been reproduced hundreds of times since; they have become as familiar as the image of Sophie with her dreadlocks and stunning smile.

On Friday March 14 Dr Naomi Carter, a general practitioner and pathologist, outlined the injuries received by the couple and, as part of her evidence, submitted the photographs. Members of the jury were visually distressed while some of the evidence was being read out, especially when it came to the catalogue of injuries sustained by both Rob and Sophie. The list recounted by Dr Carter was graphic in the extreme. She talked of seeing Sophie on August 16, five days after the attack, and her being in a 'deeply unconscious' state, breathing with the aid of a ventilator. The injuries to Sophie's brain were likened to those of a car crash victim, said consultant neuropathologist Dr Daniel de Plessis. Dr Carter said the 20-year-old had 17 injuries to her face, body and head.

One of the nurses who looked after Rob at North Manchester General Hospital said she had never witnessed such severe injuries.

A statement from a paramedic read out in court said Sophie and Rob were so badly beaten that it was impossible at first to determine whether they were male or female. Ambulance technician Neil Warburton's statement said:

"We gave her oxygen and inserted a plastic tube in her throat. She had a lot of blood all over her face and what looked like blood coming out of her ears. Her pupils were fixed in a constrictive position. This was of great concern to us. We wanted to get her to hospital as quickly as possible."

That ambulance took Sophie to Rochdale Infirmary, the nearest accident and emergency department, while a second ambulance transferred Rob to the same hospital.

It was him. Three words that sum up the evidence presented by Harris as his defence to the crime of murder. He laid the blame on Herbert who would never take the stand. And who would ever take his word? He was a confessed murderer. Answering questions from his barrister Andrew O'Byrne QC, Harris put the blame firmly on Herbert. He described how Herbert had 'volley kicked' Sophie as if she were a ball.

"Her head went back and forward. He then kicked her in the face and started stamping on her head. I tried stopping it. I ran over and pulled him off her."

He stood by his claims that he never hit her, saying he was on his mobile phone all the time the attack was taking place. Under cross-examination Mr Shorrock accused Harris of attacking Rob more than once and solely because of how he looked.

"You recall very well what you did that night and you do not want anyone to know about it. You were there until the very end. You kicked Sophie. You and Herbert caused those horrible injuries to her."

Harris continued to deny his involvement and claimed cuts found on his hands could have been caused through a summer job. He claimed all the witnesses were mistaken. He could not explain why he had finger marks on his shoulders, which another witness said had been caused by him trying to pull Harris away and stop the attack. The police had forensic evidence. Blood from Rob was found on the inner part of the left leg of Harris's trousers, supporting the view that he had been in contact with Rob's wet blood. There was no forensic evidence linking him with Sophie's attack, only eyewitness accounts. That forensic evidence contradicted Harris's own account of his involvement in the attack on Rob – he admitted grievous bodily harm with intent, and claimed to only punch Rob once.

20

Judgement day came on Thursday March 27, 2008. With the evidence concluded and the jury expected to be sent out to reach a verdict, the *Free Press* would not be able to publish the outcome until the following week. The court case made the front page but we had to go on the line that the families were anxiously waiting for a verdict. On the inside pages we carried the evidence reporters had heard in court.

As I left home to make that now all too familiar journey to Preston, I couldn't take my mind off what may happen that day. I was, hopefully, going to witness justice. In my mind there really was no doubt that the jury was going to convict after hearing the weight of evidence. How could they reach any other verdict? But I also knew that the British justice system could be unpredictable so I dare not whisper my thoughts to anyone.

Judge Russell's first task was to conclude his direction to the jury:

"If you are sure that the defendant took part in the attack on Sophie Lancaster and he did intend to kill her or cause her serious injury then he is guilty of murder. Although he was drunk at the time, provided you are sure that he actually formed the intention to kill or cause really serious injuries then he is guilty of murder.

"If, however, you are not sure that he formed the intention to kill, or cause really serious injuries, because he was so drunk that he couldn't form this intention, then provided you are sure he took part in the attack then you find him not guilty of murder but guilty of manslaughter.

"If, of course, you are not sure he took part in the attack at all and the prosecution has failed to prove its case then you should find him not guilty."

The jury retired at 11.40am and we all left the room. I immediately transcribed the judge's final summation. Surely there was only one verdict. I joined the collection of reporters in the cafe area; we filled a good number of the seats that day. When it became clear that no decision was going to be reached until after lunch, some retired to local hostelries. I stayed put. I had no intention of leaving that court building until I knew the verdict; I had made that mistake once in this case. Of the 21 years that I had lived in Rossendale and worked as a reporter, this was the biggest criminal case in the area's history. This time I had made sure there was plenty of time on the car's pay and display ticket.

At 2.10pm the usher motioned for us all to come back in. I hurriedly made sure I got a good seat at the front of the press bench, from there I could clearly see Harris, Sylvia and her supporters and the jury. The verdict was vital, but I wanted to witness their reactions, to illustrate the court report with details of the emotions, to make the readers feel that they were present at the hearing. There was so much interest it took a further 10 minutes before everyone was seated and in position. Then came the customary knock on the door and everyone was ordered: "Please stand."

The judge took centre stage and we held our pens poised waiting to hear the foreman present the jury's decision.

Although technically it had been two hours and 40 minutes since the jury had retired to consider the evidence and the options available to them, this had also included lunch and the time it took to reassemble the media.

"How do you find the defendant on the charge of murdering Sophie Lancaster?"

"Guilty."

I was confident of what I was going to hear so I made sure my eyes were trained on Harris and not on the foreman. The teen was standing in the dock flanked by security guards, dressed in a charcoal grey suit. He never moved a muscle as the verdict was announced. He gave the impression of being someone who really didn't seem bothered. From my front-row vantage point, I could also observe the public area, where once again Sylvia had been seated in the vicinity of Harris's mother, Martine. Fortunately she had Rob's mum Tracy and friends for company, as well as her family liaison officer. A distinct and very clear and loud shout of 'Yes' could be heard from the direction of Sylvia and her supporters; this cry was one of sheer relief and one that would not lead to criticism from the judge. I looked across to Sylvia and mouthed the words: "Thank God." Sylvia acknowledged my comment and burst into tears. Tracy, Rob's mum, rested her head on Sylvia's shoulder. All around me journalists hastily tapped the verdict into their mobile phones, on silent of course, but not switched off. Newsrooms were waiting anxiously for the verdict, guilty or not guilty, who would be first with the result? Life is not quite so hectic when you work for a weekly paper.

The judge immediately lifted the order that had previously banned the identification of Herbert and Harris. At last newspapers, TV and radio could print and broadcast the names and pictures of those responsible for cutting short a young life.

"It is appropriate now for people to be aware of the identities of them," he said.

Judge Russell kept in place the Section 39 Order, which banned the identification of the Hulme brothers and Mallett. This made reporting the case somewhat difficult and also led to confusion among some members of the public. They wrongly thought the three were being given some sort of special protection. Journalists were only obeying the letter of the law, which prevented the others being identified. However, Judge Russell did hint that he was considering lifting that order when he added he would 'review it on sentencing'.

As soon as the verdict was announced, Harris's mother Martine and a friend whom she had been in court with quickly headed out of the room. Although some journalists tried to follow her and track her down, she eluded them.

Mr Shorrock then dropped the bombshell the press had already been made aware of at the earlier press conference in February; it was not Herbert and Harris's first assault. The sickening similarity of this earlier attack obviously came as news to the jury and led to two female jurors breaking down in tears. It must have vindicated any members who went into the jury room convinced of Harris's guilt and made dissenters who may have considered believing Harris's 'not me' defence glad they had not led a revolt. Both Harris and Herbert had been part of a gang who had committed a similar brutal assault, which started in the same park just four months before the attack on Sophie and Rob. Again they had been drinking cider and the attack happened at around 1am.

Detective Inspector Dean Holden explained what happened.

"Last year Herbert and Harris, then both 15, were involved in an incident at Stubbylee. They chased a lad from Stubbylee Lane and when they caught up with him subjected him to an assault about a quarter-of-a-mile away from his home. Only when the lad's mother intervened did the assault stop. The lad was beaten and kicked about the head although he was not too seriously injured; he had cuts and bruises. They were convicted of affray and a Section 4 Public Order Offence and given a community service sentence. It happened in a similar location and there were other similarities, especially the violence used, kicking and stamping."

When they had appeared before Rossendale Youth Court on April 24, 2007 Herbert admitted a Section 47 assault causing actual bodily harm and was made subject to a six-month youth referral order. Harris too was subject to two six-month referral orders for assault causing actual bodily harm and affray.

On July 31, just days before Sophie and Rob were attacked, Herbert was convicted of a Section 5 Public Order Offence and given a three-month extension to his referral order.

The verdict announced, Judge Russell ordered Harris to be taken down. As he was led away from the dock he shook his head, the only emotion shown by him throughout the proceedings. Judge Russell announced that he would be issuing a written sentence and copies of his judgement would be made available to the press once he had delivered his comments. He then took time away from the proceedings to praise the conduct of the families of Sophie and Rob. He acknowledged that it must have been a 'very harrowing ordeal' for them. He also praised the four young witnesses who had called the emergency services, administered first aid to the couple and had given detailed accounts to the police.

"All acted in different ways and with commendable courage. I am going to talk to the High Sheriff of Lancashire and ask that each receives a small financial reward of £250 to show our approval of their public spiritedness."

He went on to praise the presentation of evidence before the court from the police and the Crown Prosecution Service.

"A considerable amount of hard work has gone into this case," he noted.

He asked for the names of those involved in bringing the matter before the courts so that they could be recognised officially. The counsel for all parties received praise for doing a 'first class job', especially considering the age of the witnesses. He reserved his last praise for the jury.

"You could have had no idea of the nature of the case you were called here to try. It has been most harrowing for everybody. Most of all, you have done your duty, a duty which has probably been the most important duty that a citizen of this country is asked to do."

Judge Russell invited any jury members who wished to witness the sentencing to attend court on April 28 at 10.30am. The jury was discharged and everyone left courtroom 10. The journalists made their way into the press room on the ground floor to begin hastily typing copy into laptops. The seasoned hacks from the nationals were musing over their intros, all involved the words 'Goth girl' – that label was being reinforced again.

I chose a different tack – the introduction to my story said ... A 15-year-old boy who stamped and kicked defenceless Sophie Lancaster for no other reason than she was dressed differently was today convicted of her murder ...

Not as dramatic as the 'Goth girl' tag, but factual – she wasn't a Goth.

A press conference was arranged on the steps of Preston Crown Court and the reporters quit their keyboards to join the crowd outside. Newspaper journalists, TV crews, local radio stations, they were all there, pads at the ready and cameras focused. Sylvia Lancaster stepped forward to face the media and pay tribute to her daughter; supporters flanked her.

"I stand outside this house of justice today not as Sophie's mother but as a voice, a voice that was cruelly silenced in a single mindless act. Sophie was a thoughtful, sensitive individual and she would not have wanted her death to be in vain. I hope therefore, as a society, we can use what has happened to reflect on where we are going and the changes we need to make to prevent others suffering in this way."

She thanked her family, friends, the jury and the police and the thousands of people from around the world who had sent messages of support, which she said had been 'such a comfort to me'. Her speech was followed by comments from Detective Inspector Dean Holden who reiterated that the assault had been a 'hate crime' because the couple had been targeted because of the way they were dressed.

"This attack was senseless, brutal, vicious and in my opinion very cowardly. I say cowardly because five young men attacked Rob Maltby. He offered no threat to those individuals – no retaliation, even during the initial assault. And two of that group then moved on to his girlfriend who did nothing more than try to protect Rob. We believe that she was knelt down trying to cradle his head when she was first assaulted. To my mind the actions of those five individuals were completely cowardly."

He praised the girl and two boys who stayed behind to help Sophie and Rob by making phone calls and rendering first aid, giving statements to police and then evidence in court. He said they had exhibited a 'great deal of bravery'.

Superintendent Mick Gradwell described the incident as one of the most violent he had seen.

"This was such a vicious assault on people who offered no violence."

He used his address to condemn the actions of Harris's mother whom he said was laughing while her son was waiting to be interviewed for murder. He condemned the Hulme brothers and Mallett for sniggering at Sylvia outside the court.

"Parents must take responsibility for their children. It is evident in these circumstances that the parents of the youths involved exercised no control. Something has to be done about this. While we can't classify all youth the same, there is an element that seems to find this level of violence fun and entertainment. They have actually got a level of enjoyment out of this and we have to prevent this happening. It is absolutely appalling."

21

Guilty. It would have been an easy headline to use but when your paper comes out a week after the verdict, it is no longer appropriate. Everyone already knew the outcome of the case. How could they not? It had been the talking point across the media; it had been on the *Free Press's* website for a week. I had to find the background and a new line to splash on.

I spent the whole of Friday March 28 in Bacup, visiting people, taking photographs, tracing Jonathan Smethurst and speaking to contacts about different aspects of the story. I also searched the internet where I discovered that the hate crime petition on 10 Downing Street's site was scheduled to close that same night. That same petition had led to the complaint about my behaviour at the funeral – how could I forget it? Now it provided the necessary new line for my front-page article. Ade Varney, from London, who had himself been targeted many times because of his alternative appearance, had started the petition to call for the scope of the Hate Crime Act to be widened to specifically recognise incidents such as the attack on Sophie and Rob. When his on-line petition closed at midnight that Friday it had 6,952 signatures. It vindicated the stance that Sylvia had adopted since her daughter's death and provided the *Free Press* with a new front page headline – *Murder may lead to change in law*.

Ade told me:

"I feel heartened by the positive response but obviously things do not stop merely at the wording of the law. Any move like this, which seeks to dilute prejudice with education, can only help matters in the long run. Mere wording may not seem like much but it has got people talking about what happens to alternatively dressed people every day in our society."

Ade's was just one of 20 separate Sophie-related stories in the newspaper that week. As well as the front, the paper devoted pages four through to 11 to cover every aspect of the court's verdict including background of the crime itself, the investigation and police condemnation of the attitude of parents. I wrote almost all the articles. It also contained a personal opinion column. Normally reporters do not give their opinions, merely report the facts, but this case had incensed me. I wrote:

'When you are given the precious gift of a child, responsibility as a parent does not end when that youngster becomes a teenager. This case highlights a total lack of parental responsibility, as the police have emphasised. Parents should not be letting their young teenagers roam the streets until the early hours of the morning, only to come home drunk. It also shows some people's total disregard and disrespect for the judicial system and the police. Just how serious does the crime have to get before parents accept that they are failing themselves and their children? If parents won't instil the necessary values in their offspring, who will? When I was 15 I was never allowed out much after 10pm and always to an agreed destination, like a youth club, where my parents knew where I was. I am shocked that these teenagers, described by the police officer who led the investigation as 'feral', have such scant regard for human life. The fact that Harris and Herbert carried out a similar attack four months earlier begs a question many will be asking. Why did that attack, in which police said the victim was 'beaten and kicked about the head', not merit a custodial sentence? Is it not time that his kind of behaviour was addressed quickly and swiftly by the court system? Could this tragedy have been prevented?'

I stand by every word of that column. There are so many 'whys?' in this dreadful case and I don't suppose anyone will ever be able to answer the questions people still have. When I approached my editor about doing an opinion piece he agreed, so long as it was my name that went on the views expressed. Since those comments were published I have not had any come-back, in fact many people have said they agreed with the senti-ments expressed.

As well as analysing the background to the case, the history of the park was documented. Stubbylee was originally gifted to the people of Bacup for the 'benefit and enjoyment of the inhabitants of the borough' in 1914 by Miles Ashworth of Acre Mill, Stacksteads. A plaque on a stone in the park tells the story of how Stubbylee came about. While a pleasant place during the day, at night, to me, Stubbylee Park is definitely a no-go zone. A county and borough councillor, Jimmy Eaton, regu-larly complained to me about the broken glass, empty beer cans and bottles, and the general disrespect the nighttime users showed the park. He led several calls for the area to be included in the alcohol control zone, which operates in the centre of Bacup. His pleas fell on deaf ears. Speaking about the skate park at the press conference in February, Superintendent Mick Gradwell said:

"These youths have got the best facilities they can possible give young people."

22

Where U From (Bacup). This is the title of a DVD that police issued to reporters in the court as soon as the trial ended and Harris was convicted. It showed Herbert and others performing a rap song. In June 2007, two months before the park attack, I had written about the very same recording. The film showed a collection of local youths, mostly from the Pennine Road Estate. They were walking across a zebra crossing in the town centre, in the back streets and outside a derelict former nightclub, Horaces. This was where the most damning piece of footage was filmed because it showed Herbert, and three others, brandishing sticks in a menacing fashion. Not surprisingly, this was the piece of the film that was seized upon by the national media. As well as catchy lyrics, there was also a more sinister undertone to the words, especially when it talked of 'if you mess with the gang, you go down'. The rap had been put on YouTube and when this happened, contacts in Bacup brought it to my attention. Some said they liked the tune so much they downloaded it to use it as a ring tone for their mobile phones. When I watched the video, I could understand why they had found the repetitive lyrics catchy; it also got inside my head. I was somewhat bemused by the wooden stick routine and found some of the lyrics disturbing. The video became a must-watch on

Graffiti on wall in Bacup: BTG, the Bacup Terror Group.

YouTube, notching up 7,500 hits in less than three weeks. It also sparked some choice and unrepeatable comments and spawned hatred between the rival estates of Pennine Road in Bacup and the Edgeside in Waterfoot, about three miles away. Others expressed support for the project including:

'At least the boyz got off their backsides and had a go at something positive – well done lads keep it up.'

Another wrote: 'Great vid and even better tune, keep it up.'

However some were not so keen. One added:

'I used to go to Bacup every weekend when I was younger, glad I stopped to be honest, cause if what you "sing" about is what you do, who would want to live there?'

At the time of the original story, community artists John Spedding and Ruth Evans who had created the video were interviewed. They were carrying out a larger project with social housing provider Green Vale Homes. They had been contracted to produce a heritage film of how the Pennine Estate and the town had developed, the arts project was titled *Where You're From*, and saw children interviewing elderly residents from the estate to establish how the area had changed and evolved. The film was shown at a street party in May at Sunnycrest Community Association's building in Pennine Road. Afterwards the police informed me that while the party was going on a teenager was arrested for trying to steal lead from the same community centre's roof. At that stage the centre was also home to a youth club, Area 51, and footage for the rap was taken inside the club showing a group of boys MCing and playing pool.

When my story was posted on the *Free Press* website it prompted replies from readers. One said the council should be ashamed of itself for the state of Bacup on the video.

'It is now a tip because of some of the scum the song refers to. The council is weak and hopeless, someone needs to take charge of this place because all the decent people are leaving... including me.'

Since I knew where the video originated, when the police issued the copy, I approached the community artists for their comments.

"We were doing a project on the Pennine Road Estate working with the youth to capture the history of the area," said Ruth. "It was funded by Youth Works, part of Groundwork Pennine Lancashire, and Green Vale Homes. The video was just a small part of the total project and came about because that is what the young lads from that area were into, rapping. It was a good way to relate to them and to engage them in the project. The kids themselves wrote the lyrics and John did the filming. From our point of view it was a piece of social realism. Maybe some people don't like to see their children how they really are; maybe they want to see them all acting as little angels. Before people make judgements they should try going up there and working with the youth workers. The video did spark debate between different groups."

She said the footage showing four youngsters brandishing sticks of wood was never intended to look threatening and the wood had been found on the derelict site where the film was shot.

"They were only props," said Ruth.

She called for more youth provision in the area to encourage different groups to work together.

"I really hope that if anything comes out of this it will be a bigger debate about the provision for youth in that area. They need to address what is provided and how effective is it, or is it just a token gesture?"

Other projects John and Ruth carried out in the Bacup area led to them receiving a national award for reducing anti-social behaviour. I know the artists who worked with the youths on this project and have reported on many of the community projects they have undertaken, a lot of which involve youngsters people label as 'trouble'. They try to engage them in activities and pursuits. The rap video, which was not put on YouTube by John or Ruth, was not made to glorify gang wars or violence. However other youth workers have spoken of their concern about the underlying threat of violence in the language used and the imagery, particularly the brandishing of sticks. They say this was behaviour that should have been directly challenged as inappropriate by those leading the project and should never have been filmed or published on YouTube. Rather than the rap being a way of 'engaging' youth in the project, they found its underlying message sinister.

In the meantime the Sophie fund-raising stories continued. A rock band, Dear Superstar announced they were dedicating the last concert of their UK tour to Sophie's memory. The band's lead singer Micky Satiar, lives in Rawtenstall, five miles from where the attack took place and they had not played locally in years.

"We found out about Sophie's death while we were touring Finland," he said. "We felt what had happened was so horrendous and despicable that we said at the time we had to do something to raise awareness and hopefully educate a few people."

Their gig was at Bacup Borough Football Club on April 26, two days before the sentencing. It was quickly followed by the announcement of a bowling tournament, to be held on the eve of the first anniversary of the attack. Bowler Chris Livesey told me he wanted to raise money in Sophie's memory.

"I want the bowling tournament to be a pivotal point to get people to support the campaign and raise money. Everyone who enters will bring one or two people so we could be looking at hundreds of people coming to the park. The date was the only one available in August and I know it is near to the anniversary, so I have cleared it with the family. This tournament is something that has never happened in Bacup before, but let us not forget what this is all about."

23

It seemed an incredibly long wait between the conviction in March and sentencing in April. The five were due in court on Monday April 28, so the *Free Press* decided to run an advance story on the front page of the previous week as a taster and to alert the reader that the decision was to be made three days later.

Sylvia's comments summed up the feelings of so many in the valley:

"No sentence could ever be enough. What I disagree with, is that life sentences aren't actually for life. They could be out before they are 30. Through my work, I know how the system works. The fact they were both 15 at the time and that Herbert pleaded guilty – the reality is they will still then have their lives in front of them."

Over in Whitby, the first Goth weekend of the year took place on April 26 and 27 and the highlight was the unveiling of a bench at The Whalebones in Sophie's memory. The money for the bench was raised at the festival the previous October. Sylvia attended the ceremony and unveiled a plaque which said: 'In memory of Sophie Lancaster 26 November 1986 – 24 August 2007 – an angel too soon.' Sylvia addressed the crowd of about 1,000 including a large contingent from Haslingden. Everyone who attended was asked to bring a flower and these

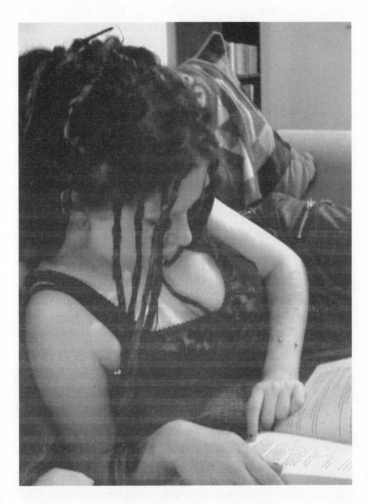

were placed in a frame near the bench. It was at this event that Sylvia met Julian Kynaston, of Yorkshire-based media and marketing agency Propaganda, which went on to promote the S.O.P.H.I.E. campaign. When I visited Whitby in August 2009 with my children we located the bench and my sons rested a while and ate their ice creams on Sophie's bench.

★

On the day of sentencing a magistrate asked to accompany me to the court because he wanted to hear the ruling of Judge Russell; it could have implications on future court hearings he would preside over. As we were early we managed to get through the security checks fairly quickly although the court was getting busy and a queue was forming outside the building. Courtroom 10 was not due to open until 10.30am but there were a lot of people in the corridor and it was obvious many were from the media. Besides reporters, there was also a large gathering of supporters of the family. Many were dressed in alternative clothing and had collected together outside the court to show solidarity with the family. Ade Varney, the author of the Downing Street petition to widen the definition of hate crime, was there. He told me most of the alternatively dressed people at court had come straight from the Whitby Goth Festival, which had been held the previous day.

"There are in excess of 40 people. We are here to show support and solidarity for the family and for the victim and to express how we feel. It is what we want to display, a silent vigil. To demonstrate noiselessly. Just to be a presence. Our presence is not meant to be threatening, just to show that we care about the family. Our first concern is that this family get through this and know we are here with them."

As soon as the court was open I claimed a seat. With my place secure, the ushers struggled to accommodate the media. In fact some sat in the public gallery while others were asked to stand outside. Six members of the jury returned to hear the verdict and alongside them on the jury bench sat Sylvia and John Lancaster. They were accompanied by her brother Adam, Nigel Lancashire, and Tracy and David Maltby, Rob's parents, along with other family and friends including Jonathan Smethurst. Ade, too, sat with the family.

Mallett was wearing a charcoal grey suit with brown shirt and dark tie while Herbert was dressed casual, as he had been on every occasion I had seen him in court. This time he sported a sweatshirt. Harris was in a charcoal suit, black shirt and striped tie while the Hulme brothers both wore charcoal suits with light brown shirts. The court was delayed because two of the defendants were late arriving from their respective young offenders' institutions. As the hearing began, Judge Anthony Russell issued a warning that anyone who misbehaved would face removal from the court or arrest. A series of pre-sentence reports were presented to the court including a statement from Rob, who was not in court. It said there had been a significant change in his behaviour and explained how he had gone from being independent with his life-plan in place to regressing to almost like a child. Rob's statement described how the attack had left him with a bald patch around the size of a 10p piece and he was now taking anti-depressants.

"I still feel guilty about what happened to Sophie and about her death. I have become much more introverted since the assault," he said in the statement.

Then a statement from his mother Tracy described how her son had gone from being fiercely independent to someone who did not want to go out and would 'go to pieces' when he was not in a 'safe environment'.

As is the nature with criminal proceedings, it was then the turn of the defence counsel to plea mitigating circumstances to try to secure the shortest possible sentence for their clients. First up was Richard Marks QC defending Herbert.

"Nobody reading the witness statements or listening to the evidence would feel anything other than a sense of outrage and indignation at the completely unprovoked and appalling violence meted out to the victims in this case. The defendant's behaviour that night was utterly unforgivable and deserves a severe punishment. By reason of his age the appropriate starting point would be one of 12 years. The question then arises the extent to which the starting point should be widened and we have to regard the aggravating and mitigating features."

He accepted the level of violence was an aggravating feature along with the fact there had been two victims, but Mr Marks said his client's age – just 15 at the time – was significantly below 18, an age when the minimum term increases. He said his client's guilty plea should also have gained him 'credit'. He added there had been a report from a psychologist, which said Herbert suffered from an autistic spectrum disorder – other leading health professionals disputed this statement. Mr Marks said his client had shown 'genuine and sincere' remorse and while in prison had written a letter expressing this but the authorities had not allowed it to be sent.

"His conduct while in custody has been regarded as exemplary," he said.

He outlined the previous offence of actual bodily harm, when he had attacked a lad who had been chased from Stubbylee Park. He described the offence as one of 'joint enterprise'.

"He did not himself participate in the attack but prevented others from going to the assistance of the victim. The victim did not need any medical attention."

Of the attack on Rob and Sophie he said:

"This was not in anyway a premeditated attack. He, and the others involved, were not out that night for a violent confrontation. It was a situation which, fuelled by drink, very quickly got out of hand. It did not involve a weapon; at the time it happened he was befuddled with drink. He did not appreciate or understand the very serious consequences."

For Harris, Andrew O'Byrne QC said:

"This case clearly has a starting point of 12 years. In mitigation, firstly the age or my client, just two months past his 15th birthday. Secondly there was no intent to kill. Dreadful though this offence was, it was committed entirely on the spur of the moment, there was no element of premeditation. Each acted together and extremely badly and viciously. The pre-sentence report acknowledges the distress Harris now feels. He has had some insight, hearing the victim impact accounts, of his actions. I recognise these words may sound hollow."

Paul Reid QC, representing Joseph Hulme, submitted a reference from his client's college. While on bail he had continued his studies at Myerscough College, near Garstang.

"For those people who know and love Joseph Hulme, for them to try to comprehend the violence of that night which has ruined the lives of so many people, the picture they have is not someone who hangs around in a gang. He is a young man working hard on a vocational course, which he has been attending since September 2007. He comes from a close family unit who have brought their children up to be respectful. Mr and Mrs Hulme can't express how they feel. They are taunted, probably irrationally but understandably, by feelings of blame and guilt. They feel let down by their sons."

He said the former grammar school student felt genuine remorse.

"He was neither the instigator nor prime mover. He cannot offer any reason why he became involved, perhaps peer influence. Young people get involved in dreadful incidents getting swept on by what is going on around them."

Mr Reid pleaded that his client's age should also have a bearing on the sentence.

Not only had Joseph Hulme been on police bail for a charge of witness intimidation, which was mentioned in the police press conference before the trial, but for some reason not mentioned in court, but the police also knew him for another incident. Both the Hulme brothers had been reported to the police after an attack on a youth in their home village. This happened about a year before Sophie's murder, but it bore a striking resemblance to what happened in Stubbylee Park. In the earlier incident the youth was hit and kicked to the ground but although the matter was reported to the police, it never led to court action because the victim decided not to press charges.

Danny Hulme had also written a letter, his counsel Anthony Cross QC told the Judge.

"When my client left his home on that Friday he was 15 years and eight months old. He had never been convicted of any criminal offence. He had not been in court for any offence and had never been warned or reprimanded. The police had never had to visit the family home. He was an ordinary young boy coming from a home encouraging good behaviour."

He said his family accepted their son was 'in no way perfect' but now they felt 'thoroughly ashamed'. He said his client was relatively industrious at school and described him as presenting a low level of risk.

Mr Cross added:

"This is a grave offence which he has committed and we accept that significant violence was used. He was part of a group using serious violence, which had serious consequences to the victim. We have to go and assess whether this defendant should be considered a serious risk."

Last to make his plea, this time for Mallett, was David Fish QC. He explained his client had gained nine GCSEs, six at grade C or above. Mr Fish said Mallett went on to study at Accrington and Rossendale College where he was he was described as 'capable' and Burnley College where his tutors described his efforts as 'excellent'.

"He was brought up by his mother. His parents separated when he was nine years old. He was quiet and helpful and dedicated to his younger brother. His pre-sentence report describes him as placid, pleasant and reserved. People are more than surprised that he involved himself in this terrible incident. He went out at 4pm to meet some friends and play football on the park. He had drunk cider with a group and they moved up to Stubbylee Park where he met others including the co-defendants. This incident of violence was not started by Mallett. He did, of course, join and he did deliver a kick to the body of Rob Maltby. He took very little part in what happened there-after."

He said he walked away from the scene and did not take part in the attack on Sophie.

"Evidence shows he played a lesser part than some of the others. He stated his intention to plead guilty at an earlier hear-ing. He is ashamed of his involvement in the assault and cannot believe the situation he finds himself in today. He has expressed genuine remorse and has apologised. He is a low-risk offender. He has, of course, committed a very serious offence but it would be extremely harsh if you take the view that he poses a danger in the future."

While his barrister was addressing the court Mallett was bit-ing his nails and showing visible signs of distress. He looked like a young, vulnerable child, petrified of what lay ahead.

"We submit he is a young man of real quality and to assess him as being dangerous and forming a significant risk in the future would be a very harsh judgement indeed."

He said Mallett suffered from celiac disease, a food intolerance. He said his client had been verbally abused while in Lancaster Farm and had lost 10−12lbs in weight. Mr Fish said Mallett was on medication for depression and panic attacks and described his vulnerability as 'very high'.

After all the statements had been made Judge Russell retired. The court reconvened at 3.15pm when he delivered his sentencing. As promised, on the conclusion, the press was given copies – all 10 pages, which had taken 45 minutes to deliver. When news of the sentences filtered out to the packed corridor applause could be heard from those waiting for news.

Judge Anthony Russell earned himself compliments when he delivered the sentence on the five teenagers. His remarks were measured and provided journalists with an incredibly powerful tool to base their reports on. It was the first time I had been presented with a written copy of a judge's remarks and the first time I have ever known the sentencing to be analysed in such minute detail. From the outset he set the scene, telling the court:

"This is a terrible case which has shocked and outraged all who have heard about it, particularly many of the decent citizens of Bacup and the surrounding area, but throughout the nation and in other countries across the globe as well."

Of the attack he said:

"It seems that it was their appearance alone which led to the attack upon them – certainly there is no other explanation which has been put forward and there is absolutely no evidence at all to suggest that they did or said anything to any of you or your group to have provoked an attack upon them – indeed quite the contrary – they were, as many of the witnesses put it 'nice' and 'sound' people, being friendly and handing out cigarettes."

He remarked on how the Goth community was peaceful and law abiding and posed no threat and merely wished to live their lives in an individual way.

"The intolerance displayed in this case is a shocking reflection of the attitudes of some of our people."

They 'savagely and mercilessly' beat Rob, Judge Russell told the court, and then Harris and Herbert began on Sophie.

"There is evidence from the witnesses that Rob Maltby's head was stamped upon and the medical evidence shows that the same thing happened to Sophie Lancaster. At least wild animals when they hunt as a pack have a legitimate reason for doing so – to obtain food – you had none and your behaviour on that night degrades humanity itself. The pain and suffering you inflicted, which will have been felt by Sophie Lancaster before she fell into her coma, and that which Rob Maltby felt both then and on recovering consciousness was extreme, resulting from your acts of violence which were brutal, cruel and merciless. The effects of what you did on that night will remain with the families forever, as so movingly expressed in the various victim impact statements and letters I have received, and were it within my powers to have those statements read out to you every day for the remainder of your lives, to remind you how cruel and wicked you were, I would do so."

He made reference to the death of father-of-three Garry Newlove, who went out of his Warrington home the day after Sophie and Rob were attacked to confront youths vandalising vehicles in the street. He was set upon by young teens and kicked to death. Judge Russell said Sophie and Rob's case was even more serious because there was no justification for the attack. The victims were not someone confronting youths.

"I am satisfied, having heard all the evidence in this case, that there was an intention by each of you to inflict severe pain and suffering over and above the intention to cause really serious injury."

Most crucial of all, he said the words the families had been praying he would use.

"This was a hate crime against these completely harmless people who were targeted because their appearance was different. This was feral thuggery of a kind that is quite unacceptable. It raises serious questions about the state of the society, which exists in this country at the beginning of a new millennium, which was heralded with such optimism. Regrettably cases where gangs of youths attack others viciously, sometimes using weapons, sometimes using their own brute force through their feet, are becoming more prevalent. Although this is the worst such case to have been heard at this court in recent years, there have been many other cases, some of them with fatal consequences, where gangs of youths have resorted to kicking helpless victims without a thought for the suffering inflicted. Where such crimes are proved, severe punishment will follow and I want the message to go out loud and clear that cowardly thugs who resort to kicking others senseless are sentencing themselves to lengthy custodial sentences."

He quoted from a statement made by Sylvia:

'Their actions are so heinous I can't bring myself to think about it. My daughter's last moments on earth must have been a living hell. Not only did she witness Rob being kicked and stamped on, but she died not knowing whether Rob lived or died after the vicious attack on him.'

Judge Russell told Herbert and Harris:

"Two of you have taken away one valuable life, damaging forever the lives of those who loved her. You have all seriously damaged the future of Rob Maltby and affected the lives of his family. Furthermore you have destroyed your own lives and affected those of your families, but you, and they, should reflect that it is you five and no one else who have brought all of this misery upon yourselves and them. The death of Sophie and the fate of Rob, and their respective families, should be forever in your consciences; if you have any."

He went on to criticise their 'swaggering manner' and the 'love you, mum' comment shouted out in court as they were taken down after admitting the attack on Rob.

"You have shown little genuine shame or remorse for your actions, and I regard the sentiments of regret you have sought to put forward to the youth offending team, and through your counsel, as hollow."

Describing the attack, he said the extent of the violence was every bit as bad as if weapons had been used. He said the brutality verged on 'cruel and sadistic behaviour' and the over-whelming odds of five against one showed them to be 'cowards of the worst kind'. Judge Russell did take into account the mitigating factor of their ages but said:

"You were all roaming the streets of Bacup late at night, drinking to excess. You were obviously out of control. Although young in years and very immature in certain respects, in others your behaviour was not that of children of your age, but very aggressive, intolerant, callous and violent which means that in my judgement you should not be treated as children."

Describing the letters and character references submitted for Herbert, Judge Russell said:

"It has to be said that your actions on this night are so far re-moved from the pictures that emerge of your character from those references that I can only conclude that when fuelled up with drink and in a gang of like-minded youths the pack men-tality took over. This means that you are unpredictable, which is worrying for the future."

Regarding Harris, Judge Russell said he remained in denial despite clear evidence. He dismissed Danny Hulme's claims that Rob was mocking or pulling faces or spitting blood at his brother, in his attempts to justify the attack.

"There is absolutely no evidence to support this – indeed all the evidence points the other way."

Before the hearing, there had been unreported speculation as to how long the sentences may be; 12 years seemed to be the expected term. So when Judge Russell announced that Herbert was to serve a minimum of 16 years and three months for Sophie's death and Harris was to serve a minimum of 18 years, there was considerable shock in the courtroom.

He told Herbert and Harris:

"The pack mentality that you displayed is, regrettably, a feature of some young defendants that come before the courts and who individually may have positive good qualities; but in certain circumstances, buoyed up by the conduct of others, that pack mentality can take over. You have displayed that characteristic in this case, which in my judgement must render you a serious danger to the public until the authorities are satisfied that you no longer have that tendency in your character. Accordingly an indefinite sentence is necessary to ensure the continuing protection of the public from you."

For Herbert and Harris he passed concurrent life sentences for the attack on Rob with a minimum of five years and 10 months. Joseph and Danny Hulme were each sentenced to be detained for public protection meaning they will only be released from their minimum sentences, again five years and 10 months, following an assessment of their behaviour in custody. Even then they would remain on licence and eligible to be recalled to custody until the Secretary of State deemed it was no longer necessary. This decision could not be taken until they had been on licence for 10 years.

Mallett was also detained for public protection and his release will be subject to identical licence conditions. Because he gave an earlier intention to plead guilty he was sentenced to a lesser four years and four months.

After each individual sentence was read out, the teenagers were taken down. Some had their heads held low. Herbert and Harris looked straight ahead, as if trying to outstare the judge. Once the defendants had been removed from court, Judge Russell offered some words of reassurance.

"The size of these sentences should not be underestimated. Herbert and Harris have been sentenced to serve minimum terms which amount to approximately the length of time they have lived to date, in Harris's case a little longer. Their release will not be automatic upon serving these terms but will be decided by the authorities and the main consideration will be whether it is safe to release them. The sentences are the equivalent determinate sentences of 32 and 36 years imprisonment – and both of them will be subject to licence, and thus subject to recall to prison for the remainder of their lives."

Judge Russell went on to comment about the police officers in the case who had also received praise from both the Lancaster and Maltby families. Their liaison officers Detective Constables Ian McLean and Philip Pilkington were recommended for recognition. Describing it as a 'first-class police operation', Judge Russell also noted the work of Detective Inspector Dean Holden saying he displayed a 'high level of professionalism which has enabled this case to proceed so effectively to its conclusion'. He was also commended for his sensitivity and compassion towards the families involved.

Other officers put forward for commendation were: Detective Constable Philip Nunn; Detective Sergeant Stuart Dixon; Detective Constable Deborah Sethi; Detective Constable Rachel Brieley; Constable Anna Chadwick and Constable Anna Kitson. Also praised was Crown Prosecution Service caseworker Timothy Brennan and both prosecuting counsel who 'deployed their considerable experience and skills in conducting this case in a most sensitive manner but efficiently and expeditiously, for which I am grateful'. Crown Prosecutor Carl Gaffney was praised by Sylvia and her comments were to be passed to the Chief Crown Prosecutor. Judge Russell also paid tribute to the defence lawyers.

"It is appropriate, in a free country, that criminals facing grave charges are represented by skilled advocates to put their cases forward as they would wish. It is also appropriate that juries and judges having considered those cases should be able to reject them as has happened here. The fact that several members of the jury in this case have returned to court today for this sentence hearing is an indication of how seriously they took their role as the jury of this important case and a reflection of their dedication to performing a major public duty."

Judge Russell's last comments were reserved for Rob.

"His courage has affected all who saw the news items and has won him many sympathisers and admirers. I hope he appreciates that Sophie's memory will be able to live on through him and that what I am sure she would want and the best way to achieve this would be for him to live the worthwhile life that he is undoubtedly capable of – notwithstanding his terrible ordeal and the grief that he will never be able to forget."

24

Judge Russell kept his word and transcripts were issued to each member of the press as soon as his summation was concluded. There was a quick dash to the few vacant chairs and desks in the pressroom on the ground floor but there was scarcely chance to write more than the first few sentences before a press conference was hurriedly arranged on the steps of the court. Facing the media was Detective Inspector Dean Holden. He calmly announced:

"I am very satisfied with the sentencing. It reflects what was a very nasty, serious offence, which the judge summed up very accurately. I am not surprised at the sentences because of the level of violence. It was a vicious, brutal and senseless event on two completely innocent people. Initially, some did tell different accounts, told lies, but when the full evidence was laid against them they opted to make 'no comment'. I have no doubt they will be reflecting on what they have done. Harris and Herbert will spend the majority of their young adult lives with that."

I was aware that, since Sophie's death, there had been a number of further assaults in Bacup. In one, a 20-year-old man from

Cumbria had been attacked outside a takeaway in Bacup and the sickening assault was captured on CCTV and shown to Rossendale Youth Court. He could clearly be seen being repeatedly kicked while on the floor. Seven teenagers, girls and boys, were responsible for the attack. When they appeared in court the case was likened to Sophie's. Two girls, aged 15 and 16, admitted affray and were sentenced to a 12-month community referral order while a 13-year-old boy and a 14-year-old girl, who also both admitted affray – each received an eight-month community referral order. In an unrelated incident, six teenagers, all aged 15 and 16, repeatedly kicked and punched a 21-year-old about the head while he was waiting for a bus in Bacup. He was also struck on the head with a brick. As a result, I posed a question to Detective Inspector Holden:

"There have been other serious incidents in Bacup since. What message should these sentences send out to other gangs in Bacup?"

"Hopefully it will be a deterrent. If you commit this level of violence you will go to prison for very long period of time."

He reiterated the judge's comments when he said that the sentence should be viewed as a punishment rather than rehabilitation. My question provided many news reporters with a new line on the story. As I headed home in the car, on the radio news the detective's comments about gangs became the headline story.

Detective Inspector Holden also spoke of his respect for the families of both of the victims. Chief Crown Prosecutor Bob Marshall praised the young witnesses who had bravely given evidence in court.

This time there was no statement on the steps from Sylvia. She was protected by a PR consultancy, Medavia, from Bristol who had contacted her and offered to represent the family and act as a buffer between them and the press. According to the company's own website Sylvia had asked them to handle the 'media frenzy' but her version of events is different.

"They rang me and offered to represent me," she said.

Not knowing what to do in the circumstances, Sylvia had agreed to their help. The company has also represented the families of victims in other high profile court cases including murdered 11-year-old Rhys Jones from Liverpool and the murdered schoolgirl Lesley Molseed who was back in the news in 2007 when Ronald Castree was convicted of her murder. Sylvia's advisor, Jack Falber, shielded her from the media and refused to permit ad hoc interviews, wanting to secure the larger media – the nationals. I was concerned it may scupper the relationship I had worked hard to build but fortunately the PR company's association with Sylvia did not last long and she was soon back fielding her own inquiries, answering questions and making statements.

After the sentencing, Sylvia, her supporters, family and friends and son Adam unveiled a huge banner for the S.O.P.H.I.E. campaign with its instantly recognisable Gothic writing. Adam read a script thanking everyone for their support and applauding the sentences.

The *Free Press* reported the sentencing in minute detail over six pages with 16 separate stories on May 2, 2008. Most detailed the comments made by the judge, which were broken into separate articles, but we also covered the fact the Sylvia had met with the-then Prime Minister Gordon Brown in a TV studio while being interviewed for GMTV.

"He came in and I asked to speak to him," she said. "We discussed anti-social behaviour and drugs and alcohol misuse in the young. He knew who I was and all about the case. He was very sympathetic."

Rossendale's then MPs Janet Anderson and Greg Pope said that they, the same as Sylvia and her supporters, were pushing to see a change in the law. The government had responded to Ade Varney's petition on 10 Downing Street's website and dealt a body blow to the campaign. The statement said:

'We do not plan to extend this [Hate Crime legislation] to include hatred against people on the basis of their appearance or sub-cultural interests. These are not intrinsic characteristics of a person and could potentially be very wide ranging including, for example allegiance to football teams – which makes this a very difficult category to legislate for.'

Both local MPs at the time had submitted an Early Day Motion before parliament to have the matter debated and discussed in the House. Mrs Anderson had previously voiced her support for the widening of the legislation but explained:

"We could not do anything until they were sentenced."

25

It had been nearly nine months since the death of Sophie and yet people in Rossendale were still passionate about what happened to her and Rob and determined that she would not be forgotten. A Rossendale Transport bus driver, Gary Thomas, made sure her name was commemorated on the highest points in United Kingdom. With his friend Nick O'Hara, he hiked up Scafell Pike in the Lake District and took with him a laminated photograph of Sophie bearing the simple words, 'Remember Sophie Lancaster'. He also placed a small bouquet of flowers on the summit's cairn. The seasoned walkers got to the top of Scafell in an amazing two hours and 10 minutes. Once there, they observed a vigil for Sophie and left the flowers and photograph.

"My reason for doing this is because of my love of mountains so I thought what a fitting tribute to Sophie to lay a spray of flowers in her name at the highest point in England. The sun was shining all day but it was extremely blustery towards the top. We met another couple while coming down. They had Sophie T-shirts on, that's how I recognised them. Alas they didn't quite make the summit, as it's tough going. I laid a spray of flowers and myself and Nick had a moment to ponder, then took in the magnificent views all around and headed back again."

He followed this in July when he scaled Ben Nevis on a six-day walking trip and then in August he stood atop Snowdon in Wales. Each time he held a moment of quiet reflection and placed flowers and a poster at the top.

May 2008 was also the first time Sylvia revealed plans to set up the Sophie Lancaster Foundation, an umbrella organisation to encompass media training, education and working with youngsters, and also raising awareness of crimes of this nature against people who followed an alternative culture and lifestyle.

A plentiful supply of fund-raising activities continued to be planned around the country with events scheduled in Accrington, Mansfield, Reading and Nottingham. I met up with Bacup student Tim Rawlinson who was putting together a documentary as part of his coursework at Hopwood Hall, a college in Rochdale where he was on a media course. He had already filmed contributions from friends who had been subject to abuse by people who challenged them purely because of their looks. He said one friend had been left with a scar after having a piercing ripped out in an attack.

"I used to hang around in that area with a lot of Goth mates and I remember a similar sort of thing happening when a girl dressed as a Goth got chased from the park."

He posted his video on YouTube.

It was announced that the Asda supermarket in Rawtenstall had chosen the SO.P.H.I.E. campaign as its charity of the year. Staff had been asked to select a cause for the store to support through fund-raisers and there was overwhelming backing for the S.O.P.H.I.E. campaign.

The *Free Press* had already publicised a fund-raiser at a tattoo parlour in Cheadle Hulme, Gods of Ink, and after visiting the event Sophie's dad John asked if a tattoo of his daughter could be inked onto his chest. It was supposed to be a private matter but when he visited the tatooists, photographers turned up and the story made several papers.

"I wanted to have a permanent picture of Sophie put there," he said. "It will help me to remember her lovely smile."

When putting the words 'Sophie tattoo' into YouTube, I discovered many people around the country had also decided to permanently mark their bodies with the striking Gothic S.O.P.H.I.E. logo.

Soon after their court appearance in April, rumours surfaced that the convicted youths were going to appeal their sentences. I contacted their local solicitors but no one would tell me anything. This was quite a contrast to the killers of Garry Newlove whose solicitors went public early with their appeal plans. His killers were given life sentences of varying minimum terms and all three appealed, only one succeeding in having his sentence cut, by two years.

On 13 June it was confirmed that all five were appealing the length of their sentences and once again the Sophie case made the front page of the *Free Press*. Understandably, Sylvia declined to comment on the announcement.

Detective Inspector Dean Holden said:

"They are entitled to appeal if their legal teams feel that the sentences are not commensurate but, in my opinion, I was pleased with the sentences and I think we would be hoping that the Court of Appeal will find in our favour."

At this stage no date had been set for the hearing. Many in

Rossendale were furious that these 'thugs' had the audacity to waste even more public money by appealing. The on-line comments in response to my story in the *Free Press* included:

'Animals don't do what these savages did. Bring back the death sentence. Why should we pay to keep such scum alive? The law should consider punishment for the parents too.'

'Have they not put the families through enough – how dare they? They chose to behave like adults, now they should accept their sentences as such. The judge was fair, by all accounts … they really got off lightly considering what they did. Let's hope the appeal court supports the sentence.'

'I pray that these animals are granted an appeal and the judges increase their sentence by 20 years.'

'Can we appeal to have their sentences lengthened?'

'How dare they? Serve your time and I hope you live a life of hell. Your sentence should be longer as well you know. You're not men, you are worse than animals.'

Sylvia announced plans to hold workshops with youth groups to teach tolerance and understanding of different and alternative subcultures. This became one of the principal cornerstones of the S.O.P.H.I.E. campaign and the Sophie Lancaster Foundation

Again, national spotlight was on the murder when ITV's *Tonight with Trevor McDonald* programme transported Sylvia on her first foreign trips – to Italy and Finland. She was filmed discussing how different countries perceive alcohol. The hard-hitting programme examined and contrasted the different attitudes across europe to underage drinking. In the UK it seems to blight so many youngsters and yet Sylvia was to discover that Britain's teen drinkers appear to be in the minority.

She said:

"Britain should learn lessons from other European countries to stop the binge drinking culture here and to try to ensure what happened to Sophie never happens again."

Teenagers in Italy were shocked to learn that alcohol was the root cause of many of their English counterparts being arrested and Sylvia discovered there was a vastly different and healthier attitude to drinking on the continent. Children were brought up being allowed to consume a small amount of wine from the age of 12; it was not considered a big issue and, as a result, older teenagers did not consider getting drunk as a rite of passage into adulthood. She also found that in Finland they have an early intervention strategy, which identifies problems and puts in measures to tackle issues before a child's behaviour gets out of hand. The programme also whisked Sylvia to Glasgow where she joined the police on the weekend beat. There she saw the shocking effects of too much alcohol in bodies not capable of coping with it. The images showed just how serious an issue binge and underage drinking was in the UK. After taking part in the show, Sylvia said:

"I think Sophie would still be alive if she had been brought up in a different country. The feedback I have had since the programme was shown has been very positive, even from my son Adam who thought it was all right; I was a bit taken aback at that. I had never been abroad and had never been on a plane and I enjoyed the experience. Now it is finished I want to concentrate on the S.O.P.H.I.E. campaign and setting up the Sophie Lancaster Foundation – I am no longer working to other people's agendas. I did the programme because I thought it would be interesting to do and it was. It also gave the campaign a platform. I just want people to take notice. We need honest debate about the issue. It is not about soundbites, it is about making a difference. It is not about me but about the campaign. I want to make what happened into a lasting legacy and through that we can make a difference."

By this stage, in June 2008, the Sophie campaign had raised £20,000 through a host of fund-raisers all over the world. That month, the *Free Press* could finally publish details of a major event in Colne where a rhythm and blues festival was held annually in August. The organisers contacted me a month before and asked if I would approach Sylvia to see whether they could dedicate their international stage to the S.O.P.H.I.E. campaign. The event is one of the largest of its kind in Europe, and has been going for 18 years and attracts visitors from all over this country and much further. The letter was forwarded to Sylvia, who readily agreed and was delighted that yet another music genre was backing the campaign. However, because the event was to be held on the anniversary of her daughter's death, not unsurprisingly, she said she would not be attending personally.

"It was a bit of a shock that they wanted to do this. It shows that people do believe in the campaign and realise that there is a need for it and I think it will be positive for the foundation to be seen at the festival. I have been overwhelmed with the support from people; I can't say thank you enough to the supporters. I have had emails from people all over the world who suffer prejudice and an international event like this will surely help to raise awareness of this problem," she said.

26

In July, as thoughts were turning towards the first anniversary of Sophie's death, it felt time to carry out an in-depth interview with Sylvia. The campaign was progressing and I felt the story should not only promote the foundation but also explain the affect her daughter's death had on so many people across the globe. It turned out to be an enlightening experience.

At that time Sylvia was still working with Connexions and was not free until later in the day and so we arranged to meet up in the evening. It was the first time I had been to her new home, another terraced house, this time in Haslingden. She was as pleasant and convivial as ever and we ended up spending more than two hours together discussing the campaign. When I left her house on 8 July it was past 10pm. Once home I started writing, finishing the 800-word piece soon after midnight. As with that first interview, I read the story to Sylvia before it went to press. All she changed was the amount raised because the fund was increasing on a daily basis. Her own comments gave me the introduction to the article when she recalled spotting a girl she did not know walking near her home wearing a black hoodie top with the S.O.P.H.I.E. logo on. This was just one of several items – vest tops, T-shirts, umbrellas, bags and the popular black rubber wristband with S.O.P.H.I.E. in white which were now being sold through the MySpace site. She told me it made her realise how much her daughter's murder had touched people.

"It is really odd to see someone wearing a top with your daughter's name on it. It is an odd feeling and you smile to yourself and think, 'Why has it touched so many people?' Because it was horrible, I presume."

She explained that the S.O.P.H.I.E. campaign was spreading across the globe and through the MySpace site they had set up a dialogue with a group in Mexico.

"They have written to us to tell us about a demonstration by young people into Emo music. They are quite persecuted over there and have taken to the streets to say enough is enough. In South Africa too they are also setting up a S.O.P.H.I.E. group because there is a lot of prejudice."

At the time of writing this book the MySpace site, set up by her family and friends, has had more than 15,000 friends and constantly receives hits from all over the world and requests from people asking to be added as a friend.

"A lot of people are messaging us and telling us about attacks that they have been subjected to and some are really quite serious. We do stress that people should contact the police and tell them about what has happened. A lot of people are coming to us who have not reported the attacks because they say, 'What is the point?' We understand that in the past the police have probably not been as aware of the issues of people being attacked because they follow an alternative culture but if people don't report incidents then the police will not realise how serious the problem is."

She explained how she had been called in to speak to police family liaison officers at Lancashire Constabulary's Hutton headquarters at Preston.

"There were 14 and I talked to them for an hour and a half

and I thought I didn't do a bad job. I was right worried and I had butterflies and then I thought don't be such a wimp! I am not very good, me, I don't like to sit down and write it down, I want to really speak from the heart."

Without doubt Sylvia's best and most passionate speeches have been just that, not prepared or written. Sylvia outlined how the Sophie Lancaster Foundation was being set up, that they had agreed a constitution, a committee with appointed officers and that they would be applying for charitable status. She had turned the most devastating experience any mother could suffer into a positive and to me she was a truly inspirational person. The foundation, she explained, was to be an umbrella organisation encompassing three separate functions.

Firstly, the S.O.P.H.I.E. campaign was to fund-raise and provide a forum for discussion, at that stage through the MySpace site and now through its own dedicated website. Registered charity status was obtained in 2009. Secondly, the foundation would be holding group work with young people to raise awareness of subcultures and an acceptance of people's right to be different. These began in October 2009 in schools in Yorkshire. Finally the foundation was to set up an information and advice service to provide training for professionals including members of the media. She spoke about how her daughter's death and the campaign had affected her personally.

"Before this I had never been in a newspaper in my life. I hate looking at myself – I think people will be sick to death of hearing about me, sometimes it is a bit scary. But it is not about me, it is about the campaign and it has taken on a life all of its own. If Sophie could see what is happening she would be gobsmacked. She wouldn't believe it. She always said she would hate to see herself on a T-shirt, so instead we have used the logo and she would have liked that."

Sylvia explained the distinctive gothic S.O.P.H.I.E. logo

was designed by family friend Ben Conboy-Greenwood, whose mum Kate has been involved with the S.O.P.H.I.E. campaign from the start.

"I love it. He did it when we started talking about holding a memorial concert for her birthday."

At that stage £22,000 had been raised, mostly through music gigs, and many more events were planned locally and throughout the UK. Sylvia revealed that Sophie's favourite skeleton vest, which was on one of the photographs released to the media, was in fact a pyjama top. It was even used on T-shirts in America.

"There was a bit of a kerfuffle because they were selling T-shirts with her face on and we soon got that stopped. Afterwards we found out that they were doing it to help pay for her medical expenses, they didn't know it was free here. They were really upset because they had done it with the best of intentions."

Although her murder was branded a 'Goth killing' by national media, Sylvia, like Rob, has always insisted her daughter was an individual, rather than fitting into a category.

"I was looking through some old photographs and she would alter every few months; she would change the way she looked. I do miss her."

Since the attack on Sophie, Sylvia had kept a diary and it included her thoughts during the 13 days her daughter spent in hospital.

"I got solace from it. No matter how you feel, you don't really tell people. I suppose because you are scared and you can't say that to people, so you write it and because you are getting your feelings down on paper, you can say what you want rather than what other people want to hear. It is a private chat with your diary."

Her diary may be published one day.

She labelled prejudice and intolerance as the new racism and hoped that what happened to Sophie would lead to a greater understanding and acceptance in all people.

The first of a series of marches was planned in Sheffield by Alicia Thompson. The parade would be a peaceful statement that people were united against attacks of this nature. Alicia, a mother of two who also has two stepchildren, said although she had not been physically harmed, she had been the victim of taunts because of her appearance.

"What happened to Sophie was really the straw that broke the camel's back. Everybody I know fell into a depression when it happened. We all know what it is like to be picked upon because you dress differently. We are shouted at and abused in the street and some people have been physically attacked. We are calling the march 'Seen and Not Heard – a parade of united souls'. Even when I have been in my jeans taking my children somewhere I have been abused because I have pink hair. People who are alternative have been suffering in silence for a long, long time. Because people have ignored it, it has carried on, carried on and carried on until what happened with Sophie and that has brought it to everyone's attention."

Similar marches were also proposed in Plymouth, Newcastle and Ipswich, and in Ireland a 16-year-old was organising an event while another was due to be held in South Africa.

"Through my MySpace page I have spoken to thousands of people like myself who are alternative and every single one of them has been abused in some way or beaten up. I went to the Peace Garden in Sheffield and this young girl of about 13 was sitting there. She was beautiful but she showed me a patch of her head where children at school had burned her because she was different."

Alicia also told me that a friend of hers in Bradford had been stabbed because he was different. Her march took place on August 31 and hundreds joined the peaceful parade. Afterwards she said:

"It was absolutely brilliant. We had a few hundred there and they marched and did the parade. We all had banners, it was indeed a parade of united souls and it celebrated cultural diversity and we were crusading for peace. One of our banners declared 'Hate is easy – love takes courage'. The biggest surprise of all is we had people aged over 75 coming up to us and saying well done."

27

August 2008 marked the first anniversary of the attack and a year since Sophie's death. Sylvia had said she was going to stay out of the media spotlight for the month and in the main, she did.

Others were still busy supporting the campaign. Bowler Chris Livesey held his fund-raising bowling match on the greens at Stubbylee Park on August 10, the eve of the anniversary of the attack. He had previously held an auction of sporting memorabilia at Bacup Borough Football Club in July to ensure that the bowling event raised a sizeable contribution to the campaign. As well as giving publicity to the event, I was asked to attend to help raise money by face-painting and devoted an afternoon to transforming a host of children and many adults into everything from tigers to aliens. Several of Sophie's friends also came along and two of them asked to be painted. Chris had secured lots of donated sporting memorabilia to be auctioned and the event netted £1,300 for the foundation with more than 250 people attending. Chris's employers J and J Ormerod also donated £1,000 to the campaign – Rob Maltby used to be an employee and his father David still worked there. Managing director Stephen Greenhalgh said:

"This was a horrendous incident which happened on our

doorstep and affected us all, not least because of David and Rob's links with the company. We felt compelled by the attitude of Sophie's family and friends who decided to take positive action."

A few weeks later I was asked to face-paint at Chris's bowling match at Stubbylee Park on the eve of the anniversary of the attack. A good friend of mine Vickke Burnside came along to help. I recognised Ronnie Nield from the Bacup Borough Football Club auction when he had agreed to be face painted and I transformed him into a green alien. He was collecting donations at the entrance to the bowling green. This time he agreed to allow me to experiment with painting his forehead with the gothic Sophie logo. I took photographs for my own face-paint portfolio and printed a copy off for Sylvia – she thought he had actually had her daughter's name tattooed on his forehead. Chris's crown green bowling tournament raised more than £3,000 for the campaign.

"I think it is safe to say that everyone enjoyed themselves while at the same time it was realised why we were there and for what reasons," he said. "I took a step back at the peak of the event and had a long hard look at everyone mingling and said to myself, 'This is exactly what a park like ours should be used for.' The police played a big part with their presence giving that added sense of security. The Britannia Coconutters came and did a performance which amazed some of the people who had travelled."

The Coconutters are a century-old Morris-type troupe who wear very distinctive costumes of black leggings, a white and red kilt, black jumper and blacked-up faces. The all-male dancers complete their look with a white 'turban'. Accompanied by members of the local Stacksteads Band, they perform a series of traditional dances clicking small pieces of wood together to beat a rhythm.

In total 64 bowlers took part from as far afield as Liverpool, Birmingham, Leeds and Huddersfield. Chris, who was playing to win for the foundation, got through to the final but then he lost out to another Rossendale resident, Andrew Cairns. However, as runner up, Chris used his prize money of £200 to swell the funds raised in Sophie's memory.

In a special celebrity challenge, Bacup Borough FC manager, Brent Peters, took on ex-Manchester United player David May. Chris refereed the game using red and yellow cards and both players were also using red and yellow bowls. The aim of the day, as well as to raise money for the Sophie Lancaster Foundation, was to reclaim Stubbylee Park as a community area. Its image had been severely tarnished after Sophie's death with some people saying they would not visit again or were too afraid to go there. This was a park that had been gifted to the public. I printed a special picture of Sophie with the campaign logo and the words 'Never Forget' and left it fastened it to the railings of the skate park. This park belonged to all of us.

The anniversary of the attack was also the trigger for Sophie's friends, Stephanie Rowe and Leanne Millar, to hold a fund-raising event of gigantic proportions – a 14,000 ft tandem parachute jump. Leanne had been pals with Sophie for three years and was also mates with Rob, and Jonathan Smethurst. Describing her, Leanne said:

"She wanted to be a friend to everyone. People have said how nice and friendly Spo [as she called Sophie] and Rob were to everyone on the night they were attacked. At the end of the day that is what got her killed; she just met the wrong friends."

When Jonathan had passed on the news that Sophie's life support machine was to be turned off, Leanne broke down.

"As a carer I knew exactly what was going to happen. I will never forget that phone call and never forget that moment, it was too horrible. I couldn't go to see her in the hospital. I wanted to remember her as she was and the good times we had together. Now I have seen the pictures of Spo and Rob, because they were released to the press, I can't get them out of my head although I support the families' decision to release the photographs and I think it was brave of them to do so. It must have been so hard for Rob, he couldn't have recognised himself or Spo from the pictures."

Stephanie, who used to live in Rossendale, and Leanne, from Bacup, both knew Sophie at different times of her life. They were sharing memories of their friend on the anniversary of the attack, when they began discussing their bucket lists – things they wanted to do before they 'kicked the bucket'.

"Stephanie said she always wanted to skydive and I said I was terrified of heights and was claustrophobic and didn't want to do it," Leanne said.

"She said if she was doing it, so was I and we decided we were both going to have to do each other's lists."

The parachute jump was arranged to coincide with what would have been Sophie's 22nd birthday and they agreed to raise money for the Sophie Lancaster Foundation, eventually raising £400 between them.

"First it was raining and so it had to be postponed. The second time they were still waiting for the weather to clear, but then the third time it was perfect. I could not believe it, it was such an amazing day and we were jumping. Every single emotion was going through me and I did think, 'What if I die while I am doing this?' But I just thought to myself if that happened then I would be with my mate and my grandad, the two people that I missed the most. That was not a bad thing. The wind rushes into your face so much when you are free falling, but there is no experience like it. I want to do it solo now! Stephanie had a huge smile on her face because we could see each other as we were descending. You free fall for two minutes and I just felt like I was flying. Blackpool Tower looked like a matchstick and the houses were so tiny. I felt really special and everyone was saying to me afterwards, 'You are a skydiver.' The best thing was that as I landed on the ground I had this big smile on my face. It was like I had achieved something, and then I thought about all the press coverage because of what we had done and how many people knew about it and the campaign. I know if Spo had still been here she would have also been in a parachute. She would have wanted to have a go, too. When I jumped I put on a pair of stripy socks. They were for Spo because that is what she would always wear. I also had my S.O.P.H.I.E. wristband and wore black eye liner for Spo, and I don't normally wear make up."

Leanne paid tribute to her friend describing her loyalty.

"I wasn't her best friend, Jonathan was, but she was just amazing. When she walked into anybody's life she changed what was happening, but not intentionally. She also had a very sensitive side that she would keep hidden sometimes. She had the sort of personality that would light up a room. She was the most loyal person I have known. If you needed to talk to her about anything, you knew that she would listen. She would never judge you and you knew that anything you discussed would be kept between you and her. My mum sent me a quote from Judy Garland. It said, 'Always be a first rate version of yourself, not a second rate version of somebody else.' That sums Spo up very well."

28

On the anniversary of the attack Sylvia received a call to say a judge had considered the application made by the five teenagers and decided they could have leave to appeal the sentences imposed. This time their counsel would plead for their sentences to be cut in front of three of the highest judges in the land at the Court of Appeal in London. Once more, the Sophie case made the front page of the *Free Press* on August 22, two days before the anniversary of her death.

Sylvia kindly rang me at home to explain what was happening, although she had not yet been given a date for the appeal.

"The timing is horrendous. It is just one more aspect of our judicial system that favours the perpetrators rather than the victim. I think they could have made a better choice of date to tell me. They could have waited until the first week in September, at least given me a grieving period. It was never going to be palatable, but it would have been better to defer informing us; for me and for Rob. I have spoken to Rob and he is not happy. I am there whenever he wants to speak to me."

Understandably she did not want to pass further comment but wanted to thank people who had donated and organised fund-raising events since her daughter's death.

"People have been fabulous. They are so kind and it actually helps you get through it. It has helped me to cope."

She explained she was to appear on the BBC's *One Show* to promote the S.O.P.H.I.E. campaign.

"It will be really interesting. They are focusing on the campaign and looking at how people react to people from alternative cultures. They will have people on the streets and will be gauging the reaction to them."

Detective Inspector Dean Holden said:

"I will be attending the hearing in London and our family liaison officers will continue to support the families. We fully appreciate the judicial system, that everybody has the right for a judge to consider whether they have grounds to appeal. I am aware that it will be quite sensitive for the members of both families and the public, but it is our judicial system."

Further fund-raisers were also being held all over the country and when the Colne Rhythm and Blues Festival dedicated its international stage to Sophie's memory it raised £1,200 for the cause. Friends of Sylvia and Sophie attended to sell wristbands and raise awareness of the foundation.

At Rawtenstall's branch of Asda a bag-packing event was held along with a tombola, raffle and lucky dips and nearly £1,200 was raised for the foundation. To coincide with the anniversary of Sophie's death, it was announced that money was being donated to the neurological unit at Salford's Hope Hospital where Sophie was cared for before her death.

Sylvia said:

"As we face the first anniversary of Sophie's death we feel a deep overwhelming sadness that such a vibrant caring young woman is no longer with us. Sophie would undoubtedly have made a difference to society. We, her family, along with friends have in the past year been involved in creating a lasting legacy to her. We have done this by establishing the Sophie Lancaster Foundation. The response and support from people in the UK and internationally has been amazing and helped us to get through what has been a traumatic and at times disturbing year. We miss Sophie every day and will work towards making a difference for others in her name."

I met Paul Mannion, from Rawtenstall, who had been a good friend of Sophie's. He had visited the park on the weekend of the anniversary of the attack and left flowers on the railings. Together with friends he had stood in quiet reflection at the ad hoc shrine at the skate park.

"It was difficult to be in the park. I couldn't cry but I couldn't smile. I stood saying nothing and this man came up who had been walking his dog. He asked if we were friends of Sophie's and then he said, 'I am sorry for your loss, try to keep your chin up.' I tapped him on the shoulder and thanked him."

He explained how much he missed his friend and added:

"This year is easier than last. We all had 13 days of agony when Sophie was in hospital. It has been different without her, there is a big hole. We are all still missing that one person that lit everybody's life up. My overriding memory of her will be her saying, 'Maz!' and hugging me."

He also revealed he was planning to celebrate what would have been her 22nd birthday by breathing fire at a fund-raising event in Burnley in November.

The date of the teenagers' appeal was set for October 7, 2008. Sylvia's comments on the appeal were succinct when she said simply:

"I just hope that justice is upheld."

That news came in the same week that a link between the Sophie Lancaster Foundation and Yorkshire-based marketing company, Propaganda, was officially announced. The company had created striking adverts using the photograph of Sophie, which was now internationally renowned, wearing her red T-shirt and matching red material wrapped around her dark dreadlocks. Of the link with Propaganda, Sylvia said:

"I was so nervous beforehand, but when I saw the work, it perfectly communicated the core message of the foundation and how I want Sophie to be remembered. For me it was really important to balance Sophie's character as a sensitive, intelligent and caring girl, proud of who she was, as well as conveying the horrendous and senseless circumstances of her murder. We have to hope that through the foundation we can change people's feelings and misunderstanding of alternative subcultures and drive out the feelings of hatred that seem to plague our society."

Julian Kynaston, chairman of Propaganda, said:

"This has simply been the hardest job we have had to do and it is impossible not to get caught up in the emotion. We could have easily used disturbing images of Sophie in hospital to generate the shock factor, but Sylvia was rightfully adamant that the campaign should be positive and peaceful. Just seeing Sophie's beautiful face both conveys the way that she lived her life and the shocking reality of what has been taken away."

In September the Labour Party conference was being held in Manchester and *The Sun* had organised a fringe meeting on a topic the paper had been pursuing for a number of months – 'Broken Britain'. Sylvia met up with the wife of Garry

Newlove, Helen. Also present was Richard Taylor whose 10-year-old son Damilola bled to death after he was attacked in London. At the meeting they put their concerns to Cherie Booth, Tony Blair's wife and a top barrister

"I was pleased to have met the other relatives and it was good to be able to talk to someone in a similar position to myself," said Sylvia. "I spoke to Cherie Booth about the judicial system and the assessments used in sentencing. I was talking to her about what happened to Sophie. Then I said to her I wanted something done about the assessment process used by the youth offending teams. I told her that they were subjective and didn't serve any real purpose."

Sylvia told her that the two who killed her daughter had been assessed as not being dangerous by just such a youth team only days before the attack on Sophie and Rob.

"I questioned Cherie about the matrix judges have to use for sentencing, and why, after such a short time, that sentence can be then subject to an appeal."

On the last week of September, a special thank you event was organised by Sylvia and her friends at Bacup Borough FC to celebrate and acknowledge all the help both families had received since the attack. I was invited to attend along with Tina Durkin. At the event, Sylvia outlined a number of lasting tributes to her daughter. At her former school, Stonefold St John's Primary School near Rising Bridge, a trophy had been introduced in her honour.

"It is the creative writing cup and will be presented every year along with a £10 book token."

Other lasting tributes included an art competition with the libraries in Rossendale and the setting up of workshops with young people.

Sylvia said one of the successes of the S.O.P.H.I.E. campaign had been to give people a voice. A recent message on the campaign's MySpace page had been from an 18-year-old boy who now said he felt able to tell the police about problems: 'Young people from all over the country are now able to stand up and say that it is not good enough and they are not standing for prejudice and intolerance any more.'

She thanked everyone who attended for their help over the year and gave a special gift to Rose Partridge who tended to the flowers on the unofficial shrine on the skate park and at Sophie's grave in Whitworth Cemetery. Sylvia had met Rose on Christmas Day at her daughter's graveside.

29

Once again the Sophie Lancaster case was to make national headlines as the appeal court sat on October 7, 2008, to hear barristers plead for their clients that their sentences were too long. Although the three judges heard hours of evidence from those representing Herbert, Harris, the Hulme brothers and Mallett, they reserved making their decision. This prolonged the agony for the family and friends of both Rob and Sophie.

I felt that in his lengthy and detailed sentencing remarks, Judge Anthony Russell had covered all bases. He was meticulous in his summary of the case and the involvement of each of the five. At the close of the Court of Appeal hearing, Lord Judge said the court had decided to take time to consider 'our judgement and our reasons in this case'.

I rang Sylvia from home that night and spoke to her in her London hotel room.

"It is quite bewildering. We had to sit there listening to five barristers speaking up for the lads and just one person was speaking up for Sophie. They made it seem like it was our Sophie's fault when they were saying how wonderful these young boys were. In court they were saying that their age should be taken into account and they were arguing that they had not used a weapon and that the severity of the crime was not enough to warrant the sentences. Harris didn't come across quite as sure. We were on a balcony and I had to stand up to hear what was being said. The decision could take 48 hours or it could take weeks, but they have said they will give us the result 48 hours ahead of it being released as an official statement. I will let you know what they decide as soon as I get it."

Sylvia said she was glad the judges were taking their time over the decision because the issues raised were very complex.

"We had a lot of support in court. There was someone from Newcastle, people from Burnley, Gloucester and a lot of people from Rossendale. Rob's mum Tracy also went to the hearing and handed in a further impact statement. Rob stayed at home."

Sylvia said she and Tracy only had to face Harris in court, as the other four were not present. She praised the support from Lancashire police officers who attended the hearing, including Chief Superintendent Neil Smith and Detective Inspector Dean Holden. I contacted the detective the next day. He was still in London, having his breakfast in the hotel, but spared the time to tell me:

"Sometimes judges decide to go away and reason it through. I think if they get a reduction, I can't see it being significant."

So Sylvia's long wait began. It was October 29 before the three judges finally released their official statement. They reduced the sentence of one of Sophie's killers, Herbert, but only by nine months, because he should have been given a greater allowance for his plea of guilty. The appeals by Harris, Mallett and the Hulme brothers were dismissed entirely.

On the front page of the *Free Press* on October 31 the headline was simply, 'Justice has been upheld'. The four simple words spoken by Sylvia summed up the verdict of those appeal court judges.

"I feel that justice, although it will never be done, has been upheld," she said. "It has been a torturous time waiting for the verdict. The reality is they did what they did. They should have stood up and taken the sentences like men instead of wasting taxpayers' money on an appeal. It proves the judge in Preston got it right and it also upholds his comments that the attack against Sophie and Rob was a hate crime. It sends out a message that we are not taking it any more; age is no defence."

The judges sitting in the Court of Appeal described the attack as 'an appalling crime' and said Sophie had shown 'remarkable courage' when she rushed to assist her boyfriend, only to be attacked herself. The court had been given new victim impact statements from Sylvia and also Rob's mother, Tracy. In her statement she said:

'Physically, he suffers from poor short-term memory and becomes very uncoordinated when tired. His balance is also poor when he is tired. Rob's main problem is psychological. He has virtually become a recluse and will not leave our home unless absolutely necessary.'

With the verdict announced, Detective Inspector Dean Holden said:

"I think this is a landmark case and will set a precedent for future sentencing. Now, up and down the country this case will be used and cited by judges when they pass sentence. We had prepared for the worst but Sylvia is over the moon. Maintaining the sentences for the majority is brilliant, particularly in relation to the sentences for the offence against Rob, which sends out a clear message. The nine months off Herbert's sentence still means he will serve a really significant sentence."

The Lord Chief Justice, Lord Judge sat with Mr Justice Owen and Mr Justice Christopher Clarke through more than two hours of legal arguments and spent more than three weeks debating their verdict.

Rossendale MP Janet Anderson added her views to the article describing the murder as a 'horrendous crime, which almost beggared belief'.

In the wake of the Court of Appeal verdict, it was announced that what would have been Sophie's 22nd birthday was going to be celebrated by a 'Make A Noise Two' gig. On November 26 at Heywood Civic Hall punk/Goth band The Damned would be headlining and had agreed to give their time for free.

"They heard about what happened to Sophie and asked if they could play," explained Sylvia. "I just think it is absolutely brilliant. They even have the same line-up that they did back in the 1980s."

Each year in Rossendale the local hospice asks for nominations for the title of 'Rossendale Woman of the Year'. I nominated Sylvia. Often the winner is someone who does a lot of work for the hospice, which like similar organisations across the country, receives no direct government funding and relies entirely on fund-raising events and people generously donating their time and money.

I nominated Sylvia because of her determination to turn a horrendous situation into a foundation that will improve people's understanding, perception and hopefully end the ignorance and intolerance that led to her daughter's death. Nominating her for the courage she had shown since Sophie's death, I wrote:

'What happened was truly horrendous, but the way Mrs Lancaster has presented herself has been admirable. The campaign that has been launched to ensure changes are made both in attitude and maybe even the law shows great courage and an

Sylvia Lancaster.

ability to see beyond her own personal tragedy. And the way that the S.O.P.H.I.E. campaign has been adopted by so many people worldwide is surely a testimony to Mrs Lancaster's determination that her daughter's death must not be in vain. While other relatives of such heartless crimes have been quick to condemn, shout and speak out, Mrs Lancaster has retained a quiet composure in the public eye. Her measured responses have not attacked the families of those responsible, but have shown an intelligent and considered reaction to what must have devastated her life and that of all those around her. It is a tragedy for anyone to lose a loved one, but for a parent to have to watch her child's last few weeks on a life support machine, knowing how she was put into that state, must have been a scenario no one could or should ever witness. Mrs Lancaster has won international support for her stoic determination to change people's attitudes towards those who only stand out because they dress differently – wasn't it true that not so long ago the same reaction was faced by people just because of the colour of their skin? Please consider Mrs Lancaster for this award because I believe she has truly shown commendable spirit to achieve a positive goal out of a truly horrific occurrence.'

As many others did, I sent in my nomination papers, and was then contacted by Kate Conboy-Greenwood to say that Sylvia had been invited to attend the Woman of the Year dinner. She was announced as the winner.

Sylvia said:

"I was really quite surprised to hear my name announced when I hadn't even thought of anything to say. It was very emotional because the S.O.P.H.I.E. campaign is something we really believe in and that is why we are doing it. You don't realise how much people actually know about it and how much notice they take. This award is a confirmation that what we are doing is right. I can only say a thank you once again for people's support, which has been amazing; it justifies the work we have been doing since Sophie's needless death. And, more importantly, I accepted the award knowing that it keeps her spirit alive."

The link with Propaganda yielded dividends for the campaign when the S.O.P.H.I.E. campaign was hooked up with national make-up company Illamasqua. The products, along with the company's profile and style, fitted in perfectly with Sophie's personality and the Sophie Lancaster Foundation. Surfers to the site can read how the range is as 'vast as your imagination' and how it offers to give users 'freedom to express yourself in a myriad of ways'. The company agreed to donate profits from two products, a best-selling black eye pencil and a four-colour eye shadow palette where the purchaser can choose the colour combination. Both products bear the unmistakable S.O.P.H.I.E. logo.

A spokesperson for the company said:

"Illamasqua stands for self-ownership and self-expression. It is a celebration of idiosyncrasies. But, above all, it is a symbol of tolerance. Illamasqua are therefore proud to support S.O.P.H.I.E. in its mission to Stamp Out Prejudice, Hatred and Intolerance Everywhere. Illamasqua also intends to develop other ways in which it can help Sylvia Lancaster and the Sophie Lancaster Foundation to promote the positive nature of different subcultures, campaign for tolerance within society and provide a lasting legacy for Sophie – a young, intelligent, caring and beautiful girl who was murdered simply because she dressed differently."

Sylvia said:

"This is a really exciting opportunity to ensure that the campaign is publicised nationwide."

Just before Christmas, Sylvia was invited for a pampering session at the company's counter in Selfridges, London. As part of the makeover, the pencil dedicated to her daughter was used. The session was recorded on DVD so that Sylvia could copy the techniques used.

"It was absolutely magical, really quite overwhelming. It was so great seeing such a connection between a brand and the alternative lifestyle that Sophie has come to represent."

She documented the visit on the inmemoryofsophie MySpace page where she added:

"To turn the corner in Selfridges and to see the black, sophisticated Illamasqua stand, based on 1920's Berlin, was very exciting. As part of the stand, Illamasqua prominently displays information about Sophie and the S.O.P.H.I.E. campaign. The staff are all alternative people who fully understand what we are working to achieve with the campaign. I was really impressed by the time, care and sensitivity of the make up artists. To be made up with make up emblazoned with the S.O.P.H.I.E. logo was very emotional. However, I am so proud to be working with such a dynamic and professional company. Having the support of Illamasqua and their team increases the credibility and enhances the profile of the campaign."

No one was quiet on what would have been Sophie's 22nd birthday – Heywood Civic Hall rocked. Five hundred people packed the main hall for The Damned. A Sophie banner was displayed behind the stage and Sylvia addressed the audience. She thanked them for their support and was also presented with

Captain Sensible wearing his S.O.P.H.I.E. band.

a cake from well-wishers, not only would it have been Sophie's birthday, it was also Sylvia's birthday as well.

Just after midnight, Kate Conboy-Greenwood led the 'make a noise minute' and said:

"We have been inundated with messages of support following all the publicity and would like to thank everyone who took part, especially the bands, all of whom gave their time freely, the team from Aquarius Sound and the staff at the venue. A year ago 'make a noise' was used as an expression that Sophie's family and friends would not stay quiet about what happened to Sophie and Rob on that shocking night in August 2007; it was an expression that said we would not let Sophie be forgotten – and one year on we are getting louder and louder."

Captain Sensible, with his trademark beret and sporting a S.O.P.H.I.E. wristband, along with the other members of The Damned, led a cacophony of sound – he even used drumsticks to beat a bucket, which a member of the group had placed over his head. They all brought home the message that no one was going to stay silent over what happened to Sophie. At the end of the gig Sophie's brother Adam, along with his girlfriend and Sophie's friends, released 22 black balloons into the night sky above Heywood while guests sang an open air *Happy Birthday* to Sophie. Rob was not present.

By this stage the campaign had raised nearly £30,000.

30

The Sophie Lancaster Foundation entered the political arena in January 2009. Sylvia took her fight for a change in the law and the widening of the hate crime legislation to Parliament. She received an invitation to the House of Commons from the-then shadow secretary of state for children, schools and families, Michael Gove. He asked her to discuss the issues surrounding 'Broken Britain' – the campaign *The Sun* had championed so vociferously – after seeing coverage of her at the Labour Party fringe conference. Before the meeting Sylvia said:

"I am taking a portfolio of what we have done so far on the Sophie Lancaster Foundation and will be talking to him about trying to get the scope of the hate crime legislation widened."

While in London, she seized the opportunity to also meet with her two local MPs at the time, Greg Pope and Janet Anderson. To keep the political balance she also got the chance to discuss the campaign with Liberal Democrat leader Nick Clegg.

Although Judge Anthony Russell made it clear in his sentencing that he had viewed the incident as a hate crime, Sylvia was determined to have statute changed to ensure that judges dealing with similar cases in the future were clear on how to sentence. A hate crime attracts a heavier sentence than an assault.

I called Sylvia in London and she explained that she felt very positive with the responses she had received from all three parties.

"I have come away thinking possibly we can change things; the support we received has been really good. People have known who I am."

She said Mr Gove had been well briefed and knew all about the campaign.

"He told me that David Cameron and the shadow cabinet were looking at getting together different people to form a committee to discuss their policies surrounding youth crime, culture and alcohol. He asked me if I would like to think about being a part of that and I am considering it. I stressed that I wouldn't want to be tied to any one party."

She also discussed changing legislation with Nick Clegg and an adjournment debate on the definition of hate crimes was mooted by Mrs Anderson and Mr Pope.

"They asked if I would get involved with an all-party forum to discuss the hate crime issue. They also said they would be meeting with Justice Secretary, Jack Straw. The fact is that judges have discretion in these cases and, as a result, we do not know the figures for hate crimes on people because they follow a different subculture."

Following her meetings with politicians, Sylvia was invited to return to London to attend a hate crime seminar looking at all aspects of the crime and she was invited to speak at workshops.

Wolverhampton band the Yah Yahs announced they were releasing a single and would be using Sophie's smiling face on the front cover. The song was dedicated to the murders of

Sophie, Rhys Jones and London's Ben Kinsella. It contained the lyric: 'How many more have to die? How many more left asking ... why? Why do they do it, when will it end? How would you feel if it was one of your friends?'

Band spokesman Crispen Giles said:

"So many young people are needlessly losing their lives on our streets and something has to be done. What is most worrying is the fact that the deaths do not make the national news anymore. We need to keep the topic in the headlines so somebody will do something to stop the killing and make the streets safe. What happened to Sophie was so sad and utterly pointless. It must have been heartbreaking for her family."

The Bloodstock Festival in Derby announced it was going to dedicate a stage to Sophie's memory. Organiser Paul Gregory said:

"It is our hope that renaming the stage will help to keep Sophie's memory alive and raise awareness to our society that this kind of behaviour will not be tolerated." As part of the event a special striking Bloodstock/S.O.P.H.I.E. band was produced.

In May, rockers Beholder launched a CD dedicated to Sophie – *Never Take Us Down* and they also headlined on the Sophie Lancaster Stage at Bloodstock. All of the proceeds from the song's sale were donated to the work of the foundation and a video of the single was available to view on the MySpace inmemoryofsophie website.

In Rossendale, Bacup Rotary Club was seeking a candidate for its 'cup of courage', and awarded it to Sylvia. She was not only presented with the trophy, but also received a cheque for £200 for the Sophie Lancaster Foundation at a presentation evening at Bacup Cricket Club

Sylvia said she felt it was her daughter who really deserved the honour, not herself, and, coincidentally, the club had considered the very same idea; awarding the honour posthumously to Sophie. Club member Chris March said:

"While Sylvia's feelings towards Bacup must be mixed, we wanted to do something to try to heal that wound. We knew Sophie and Rob because they were so distinctive and always walking around. We feel some of the pain as well, although nothing compared to how Sylvia and Rob's families must feel."

On Wednesday May 6, Sylvia was finally granted an audience with the-then Justice Secretary and local Blackburn MP Jack Straw and got her chance to put her request for a change in the law straight to the decision-maker. She did not achieve her ultimate goal but did, however, gain concessions and Mr Straw agreed that more detailed recording and documenting of such incidents was needed so that police, prosecutors and courts had statistical evidence. Sylvia said:

"I am not disappointed, I feel very positive. It just means that we have a lot more work still to do. He was not talking about a change in the actual law, but looking at ways that these crimes are reported and how the police deal with them. I still want hate crime legislation widened. Hopefully, these changes will mean people are more likely to report crimes of this nature and that can only be for the good."

The previous Friday, Sylvia had met Conservative leader David Cameron when he visited East Lancashire. He told her that use of the legislation was at the discretion of judges. That has always been one of Sylvia's major concerns because it allows a judge to make his or her own mind up on a case.

"We want it written into statute so they know exactly what tariff to set. Just because of the way someone dresses or looks is no justification for them to be attacked," she said.

As a result of her meeting with Mr Straw, that weekend

Sylvia was interviewed on BBC1's *The Politics Show*. She outlined the attack and also she got the chance to explain about the foundation. Of her television appearance, Sylvia said:

"I was pleased to have the opportunity to promote the campaign. It is a shame that there was not a lot of time. I am still determined to have the law changed so that any judge faced with a defendant charged with an attack of this nature knows the guidelines they should be working to when it comes to sentencing."

That was to be the last piece I was to write about Sylvia for the *Free Press*. On that same politics programme, a news item featured people who were complaining about the demise of their local newspaper in Salford – it was being moved into Manchester city centre as it was part of the Guardian Media Group. That was the same reason I had opted for voluntary redundancy after 21 years as a local reporter, a job I loved. The inclusion of that news item on that day was heavy with irony.

31

As part of the awareness-raising that Propaganda carried out, the company, along with the Graeme Robertson Trust, designed a competition open to advertising students across the country, to design a marketing strategy to promote the Sophie Lancaster Foundation. The trust was founded in 1991 in memory of Graeme Robertson who died from cancer. He was well known and respected for his craftsmanship, enthusiasm, leadership and ability to nurture talent within the creative direct mail, advertising and marketing industries.

To keep me informed of posts made on the internet, I had set up a 'Google Alert' on Sophie Lancaster's name. This is an invaluable tool and allows users to be aware of anyone, anywhere in the world, posting a message or blog using certain key words – obviously in this case, Sophie Lancaster. On leaving the *Free Press* I transferred this link to my home computer and, nearly three years after Sophie's death, I still receive between five and 10 daily alerts to stories, postings and messages. It was one such alert that brought this competition to my notice, and particularly to the work of graduate, Victoria Fannon. Twenty-one-year-old Victoria, from London, had just completed her creative advertising honours degree at the University of Gloucestershire and had entered the Graeme Robertson Trust

Student Awards. The brief was to create a direct response campaign for the Sophie Lancaster Foundation. The objective was to create a campaign that attracted support for the trust and its core aims and also made a lasting memory to Sophie Lancaster. The strategy had to be executed in at least three different media, one of which had to be direct marketing.

"I found the brief an exciting one," Victoria told me when she responded to my email request for a chat. "It was another great opportunity to create potentially really powerful work; also you can never enter enough advertising competitions. I was quite happy with what I ended up with, although you never know. I wish the Sophie Lancaster Foundation all the luck in accomplishing what they aim for in their future campaigning. It is a great cause. I had heard about what happened to Sophie and I remembered the national publicity the case received. When I read the brief I thought the campaign should centre on the fact that no matter what people look like on the outside, underneath we are all actually the same and there is no difference. I liked the chance to take on the brief and I felt it gave me an opportunity to practically create some wonderful work. I was interested in the campaign and I read a lot of information about Sophie. It did shock the whole of the country and had an impact on people all over the world. It is an excellent means of spreading the word about the foundation, because students will speak about what they are doing to their family and friends and that will also get people talking about the Sophie Lancaster Foundation. I really tried to get into the mind of how it must feel to be discriminated against and how serious an issue it is. I wanted my campaign to get across to people to look at the person inside, not to judge on appearances."

Victoria explained that the competition stipulated that besides the usual print media and creating a storyboard for a TV or digital advert, the organisers were looking for unique ideas. Victoria devised a clever way of getting the message across, using 'ambient gorilla masks'. These would be placed in town centres with eyeholes for people to look through. Once a person was looking through the mask, their outward appearance would differ. The charity would be mentioned as the person departed the gorilla mask. I thought this was an imaginative marketing tool to convey the campaign's message. It cleverly made the point that no matter what your appearance may be on the outside, it doesn't change the inner person.

32

Although no longer employed to write and cover the Sophie Lancaster stories, I never lost sight of the campaign. Through the internet and regular contact with Sylvia, I was kept up to date with what was happening.

The visit to Parliament in May led to Bolton Council changing its hate crime policies and Sylvia becoming a member of the government's Hate Crime Advisory Panel. A housing association in Blackburn used Sylvia to assist with the production of a DVD promoting tolerance to tenants and, like many others, I signed a petition to secure funding for the foundation from the proceeds of crime from the Lancashire Criminal Justice Board. I think it is highly appropriate that money criminals have made out of their wrongdoings should be confiscated and used to help other organisations. The foundation was an obvious choice having arisen out of a crime that affected so many and as a result the bid was successful and the Sophie Lancaster Foundation benefited by £30,000.

The Sophie story continued to make the news as the foundation was represented on the One & Other fourth plinth living artwork project in London's Trafalgar Square in the summer of 2009. Artist Antony Gormley's bizarre idea was to represent different aspects of life by having 2,400 people sitting for an hour each atop a 10ft high plinth in the shadow of Nelson's Column. The moving art project lasted 100 days in one of London's busiest tourist venues.

As November approached, what would have been Sophie's 23rd birthday neared and Sylvia informed me that something 'big' would be happening. At that stage she was not able to divulge what was planned. A couple of days before the anniversary – 26 November – she explained that Propaganda had commissioned an animation that depicted the attack in the park. *Dark Angel* was set to haunting music, *Roads* by Portishead, and used an eerie sepia colour. Following its open air screening in Manchester centre, when hundreds gathered to view the movie, emotions were understandably running very high. The short film was posted on YouTube and shown on MTV. I got a link to the YouTube site and checked out the footage for myself. Not surprisingly, my views on this film differ tremendously from Sylvia. The animation was skilful and the finished film polished but as someone who has in-depth knowledge of this case it was also inaccurate and I believe a misrepresentation of what happened that night. It shows Rob and Sophie walking alone into the park and then cuts to a gang on the skate ramps. These teenagers then chase the couple and Rob and Sophie are seen running for their lives. The film depicts them being hunted and the teenagers attack them as a pack of hounds would a fox. The attack over, the gang run off leaving their bloody bodies in the dimly lit park. Ghostly images of the couple watch the proceedings and after the attack the female 'angel' kisses a final farewell to Rob.

This film has been seen by thousands of people from around the world. Many have also added their own personal comments on the various versions posted on YouTube. They comment how shocking it is, how it made them cry, how dreadful this crime was and some, who personally know Bacup, go on to criticise and damn the town. My take on the film is somewhat different. I can appreciate the skill used in the animation, it sets a scene that is an instantly recognisable one to anyone with knowledge of Bacup as the animators have drawn the distinctive spire of the former St Saviour's Church at the gateway to Stubbylee Park. But the footage of the attack, and especially the aftermath, are untrue and in direct contrast to the evidence heard in court and the account in this book.

I added my comments about the inaccuracy to the hundreds of supporters' views. There were a couple of other dissenters and this led to a comment being posted by Kate Conboy-Greenwood. She defended the film saying it was never meant to tell the whole story but was made as part of the educational work that will be carried out with the aim of challenging hatred. However, if you read the comments made by viewers of the film, not only on the version posted by the Sophie Lancaster Foundation but the many other copies people have posted, it is evident they believe it to be an exact representation of the facts. One link to the film says it shows the 'sick truth of what really happened to poor Sophie Lancaster and her boyfriend Rob'.

They were indeed attacked and the only justification for that has been because they dressed differently. Sophie and Rob had posed while one of the girls used her mobile to try to take a photograph shortly before the attack happened. They were not hounded down and most importantly were not 'left for dead'. Three teenagers tried desperately hard to save their lives. Young witnesses who feared for their own safety bravely gave evidence to police implicating their own peer group. Children, some barely teenagers, were interviewed in court and gave statements which led to the conviction of Harris, who had denied murdering Sophie. Teenagers stayed with the couple after the attack, and called the emergency services. They took off their own clothes to stem the flow of blood. They screamed over and over again for the ambulance to come and help these two victims. In his summing up, prosecutor Mr Shorrock QC said:

"The impact of what they did that night can't be understated. I can only imagine what would have happened if they had left Sophie and Robert unconscious on the ground at that skate park."

These young people were awarded money from the courts in recognition of their bravery but thanks to artistic licence they have been erased from history. Anyone watching this film with no prior knowledge of the case could be left in no doubt: the youth of Bacup were all scum and as for the town itself – who would want to admit to living there? As the detective said, had those three calls to the ambulance service not been made there could so easily have been a double murder.

33

"When someone asks me where I'm from, I just tell them 'North Manchester'. I won't say Bacup anymore, because the next thing they say is, 'Isn't that where that Goth girl got murdered in the park?'"

Those were the comments made by a close friend who had just returned from a holiday in the Canary Islands. So there you have it, one Bacup mother 2,000 miles away from home, afraid to admit to where she comes from. Already the town was labelled as, 'the place where the boys murdered the Goth girl'. Bacup was going to become notorious for all the wrong reasons just as Hungerford will be forever linked to Michael Ryan's killing spree in 1987; Dunblane for Thomas Hamilton's primary school massacre in 1996 and Whitehaven (a place where I holiday with my family) will be known for the random murders carried out in June 2010 by Derrick Bird.

Despite the publicity since the attack, which portrayed Bacup in a very grim light, as with all towns there are a lot of good people. There is a consortium of traders and residents working to improve the town in many ways, including taking over the running of the former council greenhouses in Stubbylee Park, the same park where the attack took place. People have manufactured and sold black ribbons for the appeal and stocked the S.O.P.H.I.E. black wristbands in their hundreds. When those Sophie ribbons were being sold, a girl rushed into the Top Shop in the Rossendale village of Weir and told the owner:

"I must have a Sophie ribbon. I am going to a party and I must have one."

When Karen Thorne, who runs the village shop, told me I was stunned. Those simple loops of ribbon, that so many of us had spent hours making, had become a 'must have' item. By observing that simple act, youngsters were standing up and declaring their feelings of outrage and abhorrence at an act committed by a gang of children many of them knew. The S.O.P.H.I.E. band superseded the ribbons – without doubt these black wristbands are a more long lasting and durable statement, which is becoming worn nationally. Every morning when I get up, after my watch is fastened in position on my left arm, it is quickly followed by the S.O.P.H.I.E. band. It has become as much a part of my morning routine as having a wash and cleaning my teeth. On the rare occasion it has gone missing, it has always turned up; someone, somewhere knows it has a special significance. Even Courtney Love, the late Kurt Cobain's ex-wife and lead singer of Hole, has been pictured wearing her black S.O.P.H.I.E. band after visiting the Illamasqua make-up counter in Selfridges where the S.O.P.H.I.E. palette and eye pencil have proved so popular. The band was also evident at her interview on BBC1's *Friday Night with Jonathan Ross* and when she joined the comedian Alan Carr on the sofa for his *Chatty Man* Channel 4 programme. There is even talk of her having a guitar specially made in Sophie's honour.

★

In June 2010 Rob left Rossendale for the first time in three years and attended Affleck's Palace in Manchester for the opening of his exhibition of 15 paintings in acrylic and ink dedicated to the memory of his girlfriend. The title of his exhibition *Crimson Iris* received critical acclaim and national publicity. Any paintings sold would benefit the Sophie Lancaster Foundation. Before the exhibition opened, three paintings had already sold including one to Joe Corre the son of outlandish fashion designer Vivienne Westwood.

The killing of Sophie Lancaster left so many people asking the question – how could it have been committed in such a small place? Rossendale, or 'the valley' as it is also known, is an anomaly. You will not find it on a map because it doesn't exist. It is a catch-all name for numerous villages and the four small towns of Haslingden, Bacup, Rawtenstall and Whitworth. If you ask a local, they will say all the borough's money is spent on the other towns and if you say someone is from Rawtenstall and they're actually from Bacup, you will soon break friends. It has to be said Rossendale is unique. The traditional old colloquial names for areas, which in so many places have now died out, are still alive and thriving. Go from Rawtenstall to Loveclough, a distance of about three miles, and you pass Constablelee, Reedsholme, Crawshawbooth, Goodshaw and Goodshawfold. Many view the area as quaint and it is often perceived as having been left behind while other towns have developed and grown. It is now a commuter belt, thanks to a bypass leading to the M66. This route takes people straight from the heart of Rawtenstall and the surrounding towns into the metropolis of Manchester. The dual carriageway is often congested during the daytime valley exodus. It is also well used by criminals travelling

into Rossendale for easy pickings before making a hasty exit down the motorway.

Bacup is at the most easterly side of the Rossendale Valley. One of the oldest parts of Rossendale, Bacup emerged as a settlement following the Anglo-Saxon settlement of Britain in the Early Middle Ages, receiving its charter in 1882. The presence of the River Irwell running through the town proved a boon and soon mills were built up along its banks. The original Bacup Borough Council disappeared in 1974 when, under local government reorganisation, the new administration of Rossendale Borough Council was created. It was supposed to unite the small towns under one umbrella organisation; that may have been the principle but having lived in Rossendale for 21 years, I don't believe it worked. The main towns of Rawtenstall, Haslingden, Bacup and Whitworth, still see themselves very much as separate entities and with their own identities. Whitworth still retains its town council. Bacup is seen as the poor neighbour compared to the larger conurbations of Haslingden and Rawtenstall. The closure of the town's railway station in 1966 left congested arterial roads running along the Valley bottom connecting Bacupians with the outside world. Then came severe industrial decline with the closure of the traditional mills and familiar industries of cotton and footwear disappeared as foreign imports proved too cheap to resist. From a population in 1911 of 22,000, by 1971 it had dropped to 15,000 and was less than 13,000 in the census of 2001. Since then there has been considerable house building and a lot of newcomers, chiefly to the outlying areas of Stacksteads, Britannia, Sharneyford and Weir, which come under the Bacup banner.

English Heritage proclaimed Bacup as one of the best-preserved cotton mill towns in England. Its town centre was designated a Conservation Area in 1981 for its special architectural and historical qualities, boasting more than 60 listed buildings. At one stage the town was unofficially twinned with St George City in Utah and in 2000 the St George City Council minutes record: 'Bacup, England would like to form a sister-city relationship with St George City for the purpose of cultural exchange. Bacup's history apparently parallels that of St George because the cotton industry thrived there in Victorian England.' This link was established by Connie Boyle from St George City who now lives in Berkshire. She had bought a house in Bacup and her daughter married a Bacup man. When they visited, Connie and husband Doug fell in love with the town and its architecture and realised the towns had similar industrial roots. They arranged visits for students from Utah who helped repair damaged stone walls and benches in the town centre using traditional methods. Unfortunately the link came to an end in 2003 when one of the girls in the party was struck in the face by a local youth in a case of mistaken identity. Doug said:

"After that we just couldn't get anyone interested in coming across to Bacup."

High unemployment, crime, alcohol abuse and drug dependency has meant that any beauty in Bacup is often overshadowed and the town's decline is obvious for all to see. Investment has been ploughed in through government initiatives, £5M from the Single Regeneration Budget and ongoing millions of Elevate cash designed to improve homes and neighbourhoods. But no amount of money will change the deeply held belief that Bacup is a rough area. "Why would you want to live there?" That was the question posed to me when I chose to move to this part of Rossendale.

Bacup has several families best described as 'notorious'. Take a look through old editions of the *Free Press* and the same surnames crop up year after year, committing offences, before the courts, being jailed, released, rearrested, imprisoned.

In more than two decades as a journalist, the attack on Sophie and Rob was the most inexplicable and inexcusable act of cruelty and hatred that I had reported on. Previous killings in Rossendale of notoriety included a 74-year-old caretaker who had opted to work well into his retirement years. He was bludgeoned with an iron bar and suffered 43 injuries to his head and neck. He had discovered a burglar trying to steal goods from a mill to feed his drug habit. The robber had attacked because someone had discovered what he was doing, hence a motive. After a trial at Preston Crown Court, he was convicted of murder. There was a husband who stabbed to death the wife from whom he was separated in front of their three young children. After stabbing her six times he fled the scene. His 10-year-old daughter made the 999 phone call. In what bears a striking resemblance to the emergency calls made by teenagers in the park when Sophie and Rob were attacked, the girl and her brother followed instructions from the ambulance controller and tried in vain to save their mother's life. The ex-husband was consumed by jealously because his wife had a new relationship – by no means justification but nevertheless a motive. He fled the scene but later confessed his crime to a hotel owner in Devon. After a trial at Preston Crown Court he was cleared of murder but convicted of manslaughter.

But the murder of Sophie Lancaster was different. This was a crime that could only ever be explained by comments from fellow children in the park who said the attackers 'hated' their victims because they were different. Many people in Bacup have distanced themselves from the actions of those few. Although they are still reluctant to be quoted about the attack, they will speak 'off the record' and when they do they talk of their disbelief that such a horrific crime could have been committed on their doorstep.

"This is not Manchester or London," they say. "This is Bacup, and this sort of thing just doesn't happen here."

But it did.

Epilogue

For me there was only ever one job. I always loved writing and knew from a young age that I wanted to be a journalist. I would even write into my local newspaper, especially when they carried a front-page story that I disagreed with. I felt passionately that it was important to set the record straight. When my letter did not appear, I dismissed the paper as not wanting to hear the other side of the story. The phone went. It was the editor of the *Keighley News*. He informed 'Miss Smyth' that her letter had not been ignored and would be used the following week. And it was.

After flunking my A levels I steered myself back onto the journalism career path by completing a diploma in communication studies at Kirkcaldy College of Technology in Fife. When the murder of Sophie Lancaster happened it reminded me of my time at college. I was one of only a handful of students from England in a Scottish college and the only one in my class. That in itself was quite difficult to cope with at times; I was different to those around me. To some I was a source of intrigue. I was a biker girl with a strange accent who walked into college two weeks late with one wrist in a pot and the other bandaged and healing scars on her face. Unbeknown to the students, I had been knocked off my bike by a car driver a week before college was due to start – but they were too afraid to ask what had happened.

While at college, we watched a play written and performed by fellow students. The drama centred on tolerance. In a series of sketches, the students discussed facts about themselves but when they realised that they were different to their mates, they 'killed' them off. Ultimately the show ended with only one person left on the stage and the rest of the cast wiped out. The moral needs no explanation. It may have only been a student drama but it had a profound effect on this former student and after what happened to Sophie Lancaster, its message is clearly one that has still to be learned today. As I wrote in a condolence book in memory of Sophie – everyone is different, it is what makes us all special.

I still write, albeit often in a different format. I occasionally get paid for writing freelance stories and I am grateful that some schools pay me to cover their PR, now local reporters are not on hand to call in for weekly chats. I also run enrichment programmes in schools to produce a newspaper, which is the part of the job I most love doing. I never wanted to leave a job I was so passionate about, but more than a year on, I know I made the right decision.